Suicide and Attempted Suicide Among Children and Adolescents

DEVELOPMENTAL CLINICAL PSYCHOLOGY AND PSYCHIATRY SERIES

Series Editor: **Alan E. Kazdin**

In the Series:

Forthcoming:

Suicide and Attempted Suicide Among Children and Adolescents

Keith Hawton

Volume 5.
Developmental Clinical Psychology and Psychiatry

SAGE PUBLICATIONS
The Publishers of Professional Social Science
Beverly Hills   London   New Delhi

SAGE Publications, Inc.
2111 West Hillcrest Drive
Newbury Park, California 91320

SAGE Publications Inc.
275 South Beverly Drive
Beverly Hills
California 90212

SAGE Publications Ltd.
28 Banner Street
London EC1Y 8QE
England

SAGE PUBLICATIONS India Pvt. Ltd.
M-32 Market
Greater Kailash I
New Delhi 110 048 India

Printed in the United States of America

Library of Congress Cataloging-in-Publication Data

Hawton, Keith, 1942-
   Suicidal behavior in children and adolescents.

   (Developmental clinical psychology and psychiatry
series ; v. 5)
   Bibliography: p.
   Includes index.
   1. Children—Suicidal behavior.   2. Youth—Suicidal
behavior.   3. Adolescent psychology.   4. Suicide—
Prevention.   I. Title.   II. Series: Developmental
clinical psychology and psychiatry ; v. 5. [DNLM:
1. Suicide—in adolescence.   2. Suicide—in infancy &
childhood.   W1 DE997NC v. 5 / HV 6546 H399s]
HV6546.H39   1985   618.92'858445   85-14346
ISBN 0-8039-2522-0
ISBN 0-8039-2523-9 (pbk.)

Third Printing

CONTENTS

SERIES EDITOR'S INTRODUCTION

Interest in child development and adjustment is by no means new. Yet only recently has the study of children benefited from advances in both clinical and scientific research. Many reasons might explain the recent systematic attention to children including more pervasive advances in research in the social and biological sciences, the emergence of disciplines and subdisciplines that focus exclusively on childhood and adolescence, and greater appreciation of the impact of such influences as the family, peers, school, and many other factors on child adjustment. Apart from interest in the study of child development and adjustment for its own sake, the need to address clinical problems of adulthood naturally draws one to investigation of precursors in childhood and adolescence.

Within a relatively brief period, the study of childhood development, child psychopathology, and child mental health has evolved and proliferated considerably. In fact, several different professional journals, annual book series, and handbooks devoted entirely to the study of children and adolescents and their adjustment document the proliferation of work in the field. Although many different disciplines and specialty areas contribute to knowledge of childhood disorders, there is a paucity of resource material that presents information in an authoritative, systematic, and disseminable fashion. There is a need within the field to present latest developments and to represent different disciplines, multiple approaches to and conceptual views of the topics of childhood adjustment and maladjustment.

The Sage series, Developmental Clinical Psychology and Psychiatry, is designed to serve uniquely several needs of the field. The series encompasses individual monographs prepared by experts in the fields of clinical child psychology, child psychiatry, child development, and related disciplines. The primary focus is on childhood psychopathology, which refers broadly here to the diagnosis, assessment, treatment, and prevention of problems of children and adolescents. The scope of the series is necessarily broad because of the working assumption, if not demonstrated fact, that understanding, identifying, and treating problems of youth regrettably cannot be resolved by narrow, single discipline, and parochial conceptual views. Thus, the series draws upon multiple disciplines and diverse views within a given discipline.

The task for individual contributors is to present the latest theory and research on various topics including specific types of dysfunction, diagnostic and treatment approaches, and special problem areas that affect adjustment. Core topics within child clinical work are addressed by the series. Authors are asked to bridge potential theory and research, research and clinical practice, and current status and future directions. The goals of the series and the tasks presented to individual contributors are demanding. We have been extremely fortunate in recruiting leaders in the fields who have been able to translate their recognized scholarship and expertise into highly readable works on contemporary topics.

The present book, completed by Dr. Hawton, is devoted to the topic of suicide and attempted suicide among children and adolescents. The book is unusual in its scope and scholarship. Research is drawn from many different nations, thus providing a broad base from which conclusions are drawn. The book details multiple dimensions of suicidal behavior including the possible causes, motives, and precipitants, and personal and interpersonal consequences following suicidal attempt. Theoretical issues, clinical management, treatment, and prevention are also presented. The perspective too is broad; the book at once details the knowledge base and the limitations of what currently is known. Dr. Hawton has succeeded in elaborating a significant clinical and social problem with the highest level of scholarship, clarity, and sensitivity.

—*Alan E. Kazdin, Ph.D.*
Series Editor

ACKNOWLEDGMENTS

I am grateful to Professor Alan Kazdin for encouraging me to write this book. Many of the ideas and research findings included here have resulted from collaborative work with colleagues whose assistance I am pleased to acknowledge. These include Madeline Osborn, José Catalan, Michael Goldacre, John Bancroft, Deborah Cole, and John O'Grady. My wife provided invaluable editorial assistance. Typing of the manuscript was undertaken enthusiastically by Triona Baille and Virginia Souilah. Finally, I acknowledge with gratitude the National Center for Health Statistics in the United States, the Office of Population Censuses and Surveys in the United Kingdom, the *British Journal of Psychiatry*, and Professor A. Beck for allowing me to include official statistics and previously published research findings.

—*Keith Hawton*
Oxford, England

1

INTRODUCTION

During the past two or three decades there has been a very disturbing increase in suicidal behavior among young people, particularly adolescents. Nonfatal suicidal behavior (especially self-poisoning) among teenagers in most parts of the West has become so common that some authors have referred to it as having reached epidemic proportions. Completed suicide, always less common than nonfatal suicidal acts, has also shown a sinister increase among the young, especially older teenagers, and particularly in the United States. Suicidal behavior by children or adolescents understandably evokes dramatic emotional responses in most people, many of whom cannot comprehend how a young person can find life so awful as to wish to end it or put it seriously at risk. Accounts of such behavior in the media (and, sometimes, professional publications) are usually dramatic and often distorted. The professional involved in caring for young people is at times bound to experience strong emotions when confronted by suicidal acts. However, proper understanding of this behavior, especially if its prevention is to be seriously considered, demands objective appraisal of the available facts. This book is intended to provide a straightforward account of what is known about suicidal behavior among young people, including its management and prevention.

In this book, completed suicide and nonfatal suicidal behavior are largely considered separately. This is because they differ quite markedly in terms of risk by age and sex, in the usual predisposing factors, and in the methods used. However, they also show considerable overlap. For example, some fatal acts are not intended to end in death, and some nonfatal acts are failed serious attempts at suicide. Furthermore, once an individual has carried out a nonfatal suicidal act, the risk that he or she will eventually commit suicide is increased manyfold. However, for the sake of clarity it is important to consider these behaviors separately, before examining the associations between them, and this is the format adopted here.

Suicidologists encounter considerable semantic problems, especially when trying to describe nonfatal suicidal behavior. This is because a wide range of motivations lie behind such acts. While death is the intended outcome in some cases, in others it clearly is not. Often the motivation is complex and involves multiple reasons. Numerous terms have been coined to describe this behavior, both overall and in terms of its different types. The policy in this book has been guided by the need for clarity. Therefore, while recognizing that it is often a misnomer, the global term "attempted suicide" has been used to indicate nonfatal suicidal behavior in general. Where further clarification has been necessary in order to obtain greater precision, this is provided. For fatal suicidal acts, or completed suicide, the term "suicide" is mostly used.

The next three chapters are concerned with completed suicide. In Chapter 2 the epidemiology of suicide is considered, including the problems involved in obtaining reliable statistics, and a review of recent trends in the United States, United Kingdom, and other countries. Finally, the methods used for suicide by the young are examined, including factors that influence the choice of method. Chapter 3 contains a summary of the limited information available about contributory factors in suicide among young people, and some theories about why suicide in this age group has become more common in recent years. As noted above, the suicide of a child or adolescent always evokes emotional reactions in other people. The consequences of such suicides for family members and other people are discussed in Chapter 4, including factors that modify their reactions, and ways in which the survivors of suicide may be helped.

In Chapter 5 attention turns to attempted suicide, and in particular the epidemiology of this behavior, including recent trends in the United States, United Kingdom, and Australia. The demographic characterization of young attempters, the methods used in their attempts, and the possible contagious aspects of this behavior are also considered. In contrast to completed suicide, there is far more information available about the factors that contribute to attempted suicide among children and adolescents. Chapter 6 draws together much of this information, including the background characteristics and early experiences that may increase vulnerability to suicidal acts, and the stresses that precipitate attempts.

The motivational aspects of suicidal behavior, especially in the young, have been subject to little investigation, possibly because of the complex issues involved. Chapter 7 begins by reviewing what is known about the development of the concept of death, which is very relevant to understanding the motivation for suicidal behavior in the young. The motivation underlying actual attempts can largely only be inferred indirectly, by finding out how the acts are explained, both by attempters themselves and by other people, the circumstances in which the behavior occurs, and the premeditation involved. Chapter 7 includes a detailed examination of these aspects of understanding motivation, and ends with a theoretical model that attempts to explain suicidal behavior in children and adolescents.

Chapter 8 is concerned with the management of children and adolescents following suicide attempts. It includes details of an approach to assessment that has been well tested in clinical practice, and a summary of the main methods of treatment.

The outcome after suicide attempts by children and adolescents, including both short- and long-term outcome, is examined in Chapter 9. Outcome criteria include social and psychological adjustment, further attempts, and eventual suicide. The prevention of suicidal behavior by young people is considered in Chapter 10, drawing especially on findings explored earlier in the book. Suggestions are made concerning how preventive efforts might in future be improved.

The final chapter is a brief résumé of the rest of the book, together with some thoughts concerning future needs regarding this problem. A short list of other books that readers might find of interest is included at the end of that chapter.

2

EPIDEMIOLOGY AND NATURE OF SUICIDE AMONG CHILDREN AND ADOLESCENTS

In this chapter, the trends in suicide among young people will be examined, drawing upon findings from several parts of the world. The effects on suicide rates of race, marital status, occupation, and season of the year will also be considered. In the final section, the methods used in suicides by young people will be discussed, including examination of international differences.

GENERAL ASPECTS OF EPIDEMIOLOGY

Before considering the extent of completed suicide among children and adolescents, there are major problems of case identification that must be taken into account. These problems, which are likely to lead to serious inaccuracies in suicide rates, are in part the problems that beset researchers in the general field of suicide and in part those posed most acutely when investigating suicide in young people. These two types of problems will be considered separately.

General Problems of Ascertaining Suicide Rates

It is well recognized that deaths from suicide are likely to be underreported to a marked extent, so that official suicide statistics fail to represent the true incidence of suicide. Estimates of the extent of the discrepancy between real and official rates of suicide vary from country to country. Indeed, Douglas (1967) concluded that international comparisons of suicide rates based on official statistics are meaningless. In the United States, Dublin (1963) estimated that the real suicide rate was almost a third greater than the official figure. In Scotland, Ovenstone (1973) suggested that official Edinburgh suicide statistics represented two-thirds or less of the true rate. In Ireland, an even greater gap between real and official figures was estimated by McCarthy and Walsh (1975), who suggested that the probable suicide rate in Dublin was almost four times higher than the official rate.

Part of the source of variation between countries may result from differences in both the people who are responsible for making official verdicts concerning death and in the criteria regarded as necessary for a verdict of suicide. There is considerable international variation in the training of officials who ascertain the cause of death, in that some receive a medical training, others a legal training, and yet others a combination of the two. In determining the cause of death, it is likely that the training of the assessor will influence how he or she appraises evidence and reaches a decision. In the United States, for example, medical officials are responsible for pronouncing verdicts. In Ireland, coroners are responsible for classifying deaths, but have no specific instructions concerning the definition of suicide, whereas in England and Wales a coroner must be assured beyond all doubt that (1) the event that caused the deceased's death was self-inflicted, and that (2) there was definite intention on the deceased's part to bring about his or her own death. Death verdicts in both Ireland, and England and Wales, are public pronouncements. The situation is very different in Denmark, where medical practitioners are responsible for deciding the cause of death; they weigh all the evidence and make a privately recorded decision on the basis of likely probabilities.

Striking evidence concerning the doubtful value of official suicide statistics as a basis for international epidemiological research was obtained by Atkinson, Kessel, and Dalgaard (1975). They found that, when asked to judge the same case material, Danish coroners reported more cases of suicide than did their English counterparts. They concluded that differences in the suicide rates between the two countries might arise from differences in the criteria used to determine suicide, rather than actual differences in the number of individuals killing themselves. However, as cases in which the cause of death was often in doubt were included in this study, the results may therefore have overestimated the general differences between coroners in England and Denmark.

The variety of verdicts available to an assessor may also influence the proportion of deaths categorized as suicide. For example, in England and Wales, a verdict of undetermined cause of death is available to coroners in addition to verdicts of accidental death and suicide. In some cases this may be a compromise category for deaths that would otherwise have been classed as suicide.

Another finding by Atkinson and colleagues (1975) was that the criteria used to reach a verdict of suicide within a single country may vary. Among deaths by poisoning, which is the category most likely to give rise to misclassification (Adelstein & Mardon, 1975), they found that there was considerable variation in the proportions that were reported as "accidents," "suicides," or given an "open verdict."

Where does this leave us when it comes to trying to make comparisons over time and between countries? Comparison between official and estimated suicide rates over time suggests that in spite of these problems, crude interpretation can be based upon official statistics in that they demonstrate real fluctuations, even if the actual size of the rates may be an underestimate. More caution is necessary in making international comparisons, although some confidence can be derived from the finding by Sainsbury and Barraclough (1968) that suicide rates among first-generation immigrants of different nationalities were related more closely to the suicide rates in their respective countries of origin than to those of the indigenous population.

Problems in the Identification of Suicides Among Children and Adolescents

There are several specific aspects of suicide in young people that may lead to an even greater underreporting of suicidal deaths than in adults:

(1) The relative rarity of the event in this age group may make those responsible for determining the cause of death unlikely to consider suicide as an explanation.

(2) Even if suicide is considered a possibility, the widely held belief that small children rarely commit suicide may mean that there is a greater tendency

for deaths in this age group to be mistakenly reported as accidental. Subsequent suicide statistics will therefore confirm the belief that suicide is uncommon in children.

(3) Those responsible for reporting suicides may be, consciously or unconsciously, concerned to protect other individuals from the distress that a verdict of suicide may cause. Parents are particularly liable to feel not only grieved but guilty about the suicide of a young son or daughter (see Chapter 4), and the death may be reported as accidental or of undetermined cause in order to protect their feelings.

(4) The predominant religious beliefs of a country or society are also likely to be important. For example, the Roman Catholic Church regards suicide as a mortal sin, and so officials in predominantly Catholic countries such as Italy and Ireland may be less likely to believe that a person has committed suicide than in predominantly Protestant countries. This difference may be most marked in relation of the deaths of young people. On the other hand, some religions have a completely different philosophy about suicide and there may be more willingness to consider and report suicide as the cause of death, even in young people.

In the next section, in which recent trends in suicide rates among the young are considered, it is most important to bear in mind the many problems concerning suicide statistics that have been discussed above.

PATTERNS AND TRENDS IN
SUICIDE RATES AMONG YOUNG PEOPLE

In addition to inaccuracies in the identification of cases, the classification of suicides with respect to age often makes it difficult to ascertain and directly compare suicide rates among young people. For example, the age groups within which suicide rates are reported not only vary from country to country, but may vary over time within the same country. Rates may be reported in five-year age bands, or ten-year age bands; this is a particular problem among adolescents, who are often combined with young adults in a 15 to 24 year-old category for the purposes of suicide statistics. A further important point is that fluctuations in suicide rates may be unreliable when few children commit suicide each year; this is especially likely in countries with small populations, such as Hungary and Austria.

With these difficulties of interpretation in mind, the recent trends in suicide among young people in four geographical areas, North America, Europe, Australia, and the Far East, will now be reviewed. Where the information is available, comparison will be made with trends in suicide among adults.

North America

United States

The suicide rate among *older adolescents* in the United States rose considerably during the 1960s and 1970s (Figure 2.1). Between 1960 and 1975, rates among 20 to 24 year olds rose by 130%. Since 1975, the rates in this age group have remained relatively stable. Holinger noted in 1978 that suicide was the third leading cause of death among 15 to 24 year olds in the United States, behind only accidents and homicide. This was still true in 1981 (National Center for Health Statistics, 1984).

Looking at the teenage years, it is interesting to note that suicide rates among 15 to 19 year olds were high at the very beginning of the century, but they then fell and stayed moderately low until the early 1960s (Seiden, 1969). Since 1960, the suicide rates among 15 to 19 year olds have steadily increased (Figure 2.1) from 3.6 per 100,000 in 1960 to 8.7 per 100,000 in 1981, an increase of 142%. The rates for boys (Figure 2.2) have showed the most marked change (5.6 to 13.6 per 100,000; +143%), the increase being especially noticeable, as can be seen in Table 2.1, among white males (+161% compared with +112% in nonwhite males). Rates in girls (Figure 2.2) rose from 1.6 to 3.6 per 100,000 (+125%), the increase again being more marked among whites (+138%) than among nonwhites (+47%), as can be seen in Table 2.2. The overall increase in the U.S. suicide rates for all ages between 1960 and 1981, although not marked (10.6 to 12.0 per 100,000; +13%), was largely explained by increases in the 15 to 19 and 20 to 24 year age groups. By 1981 there was an annual total of 5161 deaths by suicide among 15 to 24 year olds (National Center for Health Statistics, 1984)

Shaffer and Fisher's (1981) survey of suicides committed in 1978 showed that among 15 to 19 year olds suicide represented almost 8% of all deaths in this age group. In absolute terms, this meant that 1686 adolescents between the ages of 15 and 19 committed suicide in the United States during 1978. On the basis of these figures, Shaffer suggested that suicide was not "a major public health problem." In

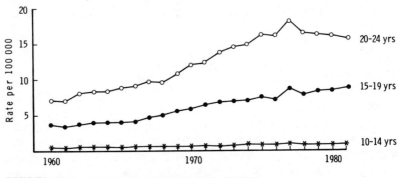

SOURCE: National Center for Health Statistics (1984).

Figure 2.1 Suicide rates (per 100,000) for 10 to 14 year olds, 15 to 19 year olds, and 20 to 24 year olds in the United States, 1960-1981.

support of this assertion he reported that, although adolescents aged 15 to 19 constituted 10% of the total population, they accounted for little over 6% of all suicides. However, as adolescents are less likely than other age groups to die from other causes, a comparison of this sort is not an adequate method of evaluating the public health problem caused by suicide. The fact that, as noted earlier, it represents the third commonest cause of death amongst American adolescents suggests that while suicide is less common than among the rest of the population, *within this age group* it poses a serious problem.

Suicide rates among *younger adolescents* (aged 10 to 14) have shown a small increase over recent years but are much lower than those among older adolescents (Figure 2.1). For example, in 1978, the incidence of suicide among 10 to 14 year olds was 0.8 per 100,000, one-ninth of the rate among 15 to 19 year olds. In the younger age group, suicide accounted for only 2.4% of deaths, and, although these young people represented 8.5% of the total population, they accounted for only 0.5% of all suicides in the United States. In 1978, in absolute terms, 117 boys and 34 girls between 10 and 14 years of age committed suicide. Only two children under the age of ten were recorded as having committed suicide in that year. By 1981, a similar overall number of suicidal deaths (167) had occurred among children and young adolescents (5 to 14 years),

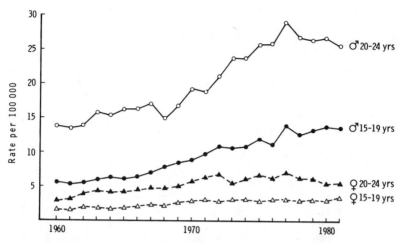

SOURCE: National Center for Health Statistics (1984).

Figure 2.2 Suicide rates (per 100,000) for males and females aged 15 to 19 years and 20 to 24 years in the United States, 1960-1981.

only four of these individuals being under the age of ten (National Center for Health Statistics, 1984).

In summary, therefore, in the United States during the 1960s and 1970s, there was a very serious increase in deaths by suicide among older teenagers and those in their early twenties, this being more marked among males than females, and among whites as compared with nonwhites. By contrast, the suicide rate among children and young teenagers has been far lower than in the older groups, and has risen much less markedly.

Canada

A steady and substantial increase in suicide rates among 15 to 19 year olds and 20 to 24 year olds in Alberta between 1951 and 1976 was identified by Hellon and Solomon (1980). In 1976 the rate among 15 to 19 year olds was 12.5 times, and the rate for 20 to 24 year olds 3.7 times, those recorded in 1951. The most marked increases were among young males, although substantial changes were also found in young females. The authors postulated that the profound alterations in social

TABLE 2.1

Suicide Rates (per 100,000) for Young White and Nonwhite Males
in the United States by Age Group, 1960-1981

| | 10-14 years | | 15-19 years | | 20-24 years | |
	Whites	Nonwhites	Whites	Nonwhites	Whites	Nonwhites
1960	1.0	0.2	5.9	3.4	11.9	7.8
1965	1.0	0.5	6.2	5.3	13.8	13.2
1970	1.1	0.3	9.4	5.4	19.3	19.4
1975	1.4	0.2	12.9	6.9	26.3	23.1
1981	1.4	0.3	14.9	7.2	26.8	18.4

SOURCE: National Center for Health Statistics (1984).

TABLE 2.2

Suicide Rates (per 100,000) for Young White and Nonwhite
Females in the United States, by Age Group, 1960-1981

| | 10-14 years | | 15-19 years | | 20-24 years | |
	Whites	Nonwhites	Whites	Nonwhites	Whites	Nonwhites
1960	0.2	–	1.6	1.5	3.1	1.6
1965	0.1	0.2	1.8	2.4	4.3	3.8
1970	0.3	0.4	2.9	2.9	5.7	5.5
1975	0.4	0.3	3.1	2.1	6.8	5.9
1981	0.6	0.3	3.8	2.2	5.9	3.8

SOURCE: National Center for Health Statistics (1984).

and economic conditions in Alberta during this period may have caused increased pressures to succeed, broken homes, and parental rejection, and hence produced these very considerable changes. However, in a companion study employing cohort analysis, a method that examines rates within the same age cohorts over time, Solomon and Hellon (1980) demonstrated that between 1951 and 1976 the suicide rate in each successive cohort began at a higher level than in the previous cohort and thereafter steadily increased as the cohort aged. The worrying implication of this finding, which was largely replicated by Murphy and Wetzel (1980) for the whole of the United States, is that, whatever the cause, increasing suicide rates in the young may eventually be reflected by an increase in suicide among adults.

The increase in suicidal rates among the young in Alberta was not just a local finding; suicide rates among 10 to 24 year olds in Ontario rose by 42% between 1971 and 1977, the figure becoming 32% when adjustment was made for the local population increase (Garfinkel & Golombek, 1983).

Europe

United Kingdom

Death statistics are reported for England and Wales separately from the rest of the United Kingdom, and only these will be considered here. Among young people the numbers of suicides increases with age, with a marked male to female ratio (Figure 2.3). In all age groups the rates are noticeably lower than those reported in the United States, especially for males.

The numbers of official suicides among *children under 15 years of age* are small, having averaged around five per year since the early 1940s. There has, however, been a relative decline in the rates of suicide in this age group for boys and a corresponding increase in rates for girls (McClure, 1984). When undetermined deaths and accidental deaths due to poisoning are considered, a different picture emerges, suggesting that there may have been an increase in suicides in this age group that is not revealed by official suicide statistics (see below).

Suicide rates among 15 to 19 year olds in England and Wales have fluctuated since the early 1950s, although these variations have been much less marked than in the United States. There was a fairly steady increase in rates for both sexes until the mid-1960s (Figure 2.3), then a decline, particularly among boys, until the mid-1970s, since when the rates have increased somewhat among boys. By 1983 the rates for boys were considerably higher, and the rates for girls slightly higher, than the rates in the early 1950s. At all times, the numbers of suicides by boys have outnumbered those by girls.

A roughly similar pattern has occurred for 20-24 year olds (Figure 2.3). However, the absolute rates for 20-24 year olds of both sexes have usually been at least double those among 15-19 year olds.

These findings for young people must be considered against a background of suicide rates for persons of all ages having steadily declined from 1963 until 1976, and then having shown a steady increase until 1983 (Office of Population Censuses and Surveys, 1974-1982; Registrar General, 1963-1973).

As mentioned earlier in this chapter, there is a strong likelihood that official suicide statistics conceal suicidal deaths in all age groups, but especially among the young. McClure (1984) examined deaths classified as "undetermined" or "accidental" due to poisoning. He found that in the 10 to 14 year age group there had been a very marked increase in

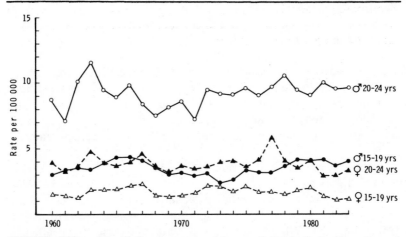

SOURCE: Office of Population Censuses and Surveys (1974-1982; Registrar General, 1960-1973). British Crown copyright; reproduced with permission of the Controller of Her Majesty's Stationery Office.

Figure 2.3   Suicide rates (per 100,000) for 15 to 19 year olds and 20 to 24 year olds, by sex, in England and Wales, 1960-1983.

deaths in these categories between 1951 and 1980, the increase being fivefold when the decades 1951 to 1960 and 1971 to 1980 were compared. There has also been an increase in deaths in these categories among 15 to 19 year olds, especially girls. When McClure added deaths in these categories to the official suicide figures to create an "estimated" suicide figure, and then compared the changes in the rates of estimated suicide between 1968-1970 and 1978-1980, he found that, whereas there was virtually no change in these rates for persons of all ages, considerable increases in these rates had occurred for young persons, especially 10 to 14 year olds and 15 to 19 year old girls. The ratio of undetermined deaths to suicide also showed a considerable age difference. In 1980, the ratio was 0.35 to 1 for all ages, 0.54 to 1 among 15 to 19 year olds, and 4 to 1 among 10 to 14 year olds.

Therefore, although the suicide rate among young people in the United Kingdom is far lower than among adults (McClure, 1984), it is likely that the rates among the young have, in recent years, increased more substantially than reflected by official suicide statistics and that this increase is mostly due to self-poisoning with drugs. This parallels the vast increase in attempted suicide by self-poisoning, which is discussed in Chapter 5. This, therefore, raises the question of whether some of the suicides are the results of increased availability to the young of relatively dangerous substances, such as paracetamol (Acetaminophen) and tricyclic antidepressants.

Other European Countries

In 1975, Brooke reported that suicide was the second or third leading cause of death in 15 to 24 year olds in several European countries, with the rates for males generally being higher than those for females. Especially high rates were reported for Hungary, a country that also has a very high adult suicide rate. As in the United States, increases in suicide rates among both males and females in the 15 to 24 year age group have occurred in Europe, according to comparisons for the years 1968-1970 with 1975-1977 made by Davidson and Choquet (1981) for France, Austria, Belgium, Denmark, Norway, Sweden, Switzerland, Germany, and Holland. The rates for the United States in 1975-1977 were equivalent to approximately the average rate in these European countries, with Austria, Switzerland, and Germany having considerably higher rates of suicide than the United States among 15 to 24 year olds, and Holland (and the United Kingdom) having much lower rates.

Australia

The marked increase in suicide rates among the young that occurred in the United States and many other countries in the northern hemisphere during the 1950s and 1960s also had its parallel in Australia. Oliver and Hetzel (1973) reported a 70% increase in suicidal deaths among 10 to 24 year olds between 1952 and 1969, the rates increasing from 5.9 to 7.3 per 100,000 among males and from 1.2 to 2.8 per 100,000 among females. Further increases in suicide rates occurred among 15 to 19 year olds between 1971 and 1979, more noticeably among males than females. Between 1976 and 1979, the rates for males in this age group were 11.1 per 100,000, and for females, 3.3 per 100,000. Cohort analysis of the kind carried out in Canada and the United States has confirmed the sequential cohort effect in Australia, at least for older adolescents and young adults, especially males (Goldney & Katsikitis, 1983).

As elsewhere, the suicide rates for younger adolescents are far lower than among older adolescents. Kosky (1982) reported a mean annual rate for 5 to 14 year olds in Western Australia of about 3 per 100,000, a figure that is somewhat higher than those from both the United States and the United Kingdom.

Far East

Japan is one of the few Eastern countries for which long-term suicide statistics are available. They show that, among both young males and young females, Japanese rates are as great as, or even greater than, those of the European countries with the highest incidence of suicide. Thus, in 1962-1963, Japan's suicide rate was 23.9 per 100,000 among males aged 15 to 24, and 19.7 per 100,000 among females of the same age. Interestingly, however, these figures represented substantial reductions compared with the rates of ten years previously, the rate for males having fallen by 36% and for females by 19% (Seiden, 1969). The reasons for this decrease are unclear; it may represent a real fall in the number of young people trying to kill themselves, or it may reflect a postwar improvement in Japanese medical services, resulting in the resuscitation of a greater proportion of attempted suicides. Nevertheless, even in 1973, the suicide rates for 15 to 24 year olds, at 16.5 per 100,000, were higher than in the United States or any European country (Igu, 1981).

There appear to be few suicide statistics available for other Far Eastern countries, except Singapore, where, in 1977, the suicide rate among adolescents of both sexes aged 10 to 19 was reported to be 3.7 per 100,000, suicide constituting 5% of all male deaths and 7% of all female deaths in this age group (Chia, 1979). According to Hassan (1983), the suicide rates for 15 to 19 year olds in Singapore had remained fairly stable between 1957 and 1970, and those of 10 to 14 year olds had actually declined. An interesting feature of suicide rates among the young in Singapore is the similarity between the rates for males and females: There is a much smaller male to female ratio than both in the West and in older age groups in Singapore. The ratio was even reversed in some years (Chia, 1979).

Race

Considerable information about the relationship between race and suicide in the young comes from the United States (see Tables 2.1 and

2.2). In the early 1960s, there were rather more white than nonwhite suicides. In 1960, for example, the ratio of white to nonwhite teenage (15-19 years) suicide rates was 1.6 to 1, and this was slightly higher among boys than girls. Although by 1970 there had been some reversal of this pattern, the more rapid increase in suicide rates among whites had by 1981 led to an inflation in the white to nonwhite ratio, to almost 2 to 1 (National Center for Health Statistics, 1984).

An interesting and challenging interpretation of these findings has been presented by Shaffer and Fisher (1981). They considered two possible explanations for the relative protection of young blacks (who make up most of the nonwhites) from suicide. The first was that the high rates of outwardly directed aggression among blacks might decrease the extent to which aggression is directed inwardly, thus reducing the risk of both depression and suicidal behavior. However, Shaffer and Fisher rejected this explanation because, first, antisocial behavior is a common precursor of childhood suicide (Shaffer, 1974). Second, depression is common among delinquent adolescents (Chiles, Miller, & Cox, 1980), and, third, blacks who attempt suicide are more likely to have been in trouble with the law than are whites who make attempts (Breed, 1970). Their second hypothesis was that although blacks probably face more social stress than do whites, suicidal behavior might be less socially sanctioned among blacks than among whites and the former might also have more effective social support systems. While noting the possible effects of cultural attitudes to suicide on the official reporting of suicides, Shaffer and Fisher found that suicide rates in young blacks were lower among black populations reared in a traditional southern states setting than among those living in the northern states, who may have been subject to deculturalization. While it is difficult to prove this hypothesis conclusively, it warrants further investigation, perhaps by examination of attitudes to suicidal behavior among different black (and also white) populations.

Other ethnic groups that have been studied include North American Indians. The suicide rate among both adolescents and adults in this group has been reported to be greater than the national average and to be on the increase (U.S. Department of Health, Education and Welfare, 1973), exceeding the general rate among 15 to 24 year olds by a factor of five. However, rates have been found to vary greatly between different Indian reservations, and, as discussed in the next chapter, to be strongly associated with the extent of social problems on these reservations.

Chia (1979) reported that suicide rates among young people in Singapore varied markedly in the various ethnic groups, with Indians having the highest rate (6.1 per 100,000), followed by the Chinese (3.3) and the Malay (1.1). Unfortunately, Chia did not attempt to explain this finding.

Marital Status

Although only a small proportion of adolescents are married, they appear more likely to commit suicide than other young people. For example, in 15 to 19 year old boys in the United States the suicide rate is approximately 1.5 times greater among the married than the unmarried. Married girls in the same age group have a rate that is 1.7 times higher than that of unmarried girls (Petzel & Cline, 1978). This contrasts strongly with the suicide rates among married persons in other age groups, which are, on the whole, lower than those for single or divorced people, though not those for widows and widowers (Kreitman, 1977). This finding is likely to be related to the fact that teenage marriages commonly represent a hastily considered escape from unsupportive family backgrounds and that such marriages often rapidly encounter major problems.

Occupation

Little information is available concerning the effects of unemployment on suicide rates among older teenagers. Although one would expect that unemployment would be associated with an increased risk of suicide, as is the case among adults (Brenner & Mooney, 1983) Garfinkel and Golombek (1983) suggested that the opposite applied among young suicides in Ontario. This requires further investigation, especially in view of the recent escalation in unemployment levels in many Western countries. Certainly it is not in keeping with evidence that suicidal ideas are more common among unemployed than employed young people (Francis, 1984).

By contrast to employment status, there has been extensive investigation of suicide rates among university students. Perhaps this is the result of the special concern caused by student suicides, partly because of the horror that may be felt by the public at the waste of potential, and partly because the universities may be seen as being at fault, especially in terms of the academic pressures they exert. Studies from the United Kingdom have all suggested higher suicide rates among students at Oxford and Cambridge Universities than among both students at other universities and other young people. Extremely high rates were reported for Oxford and Cambridge students between 1945 and 1955 (Carpenter, 1959). A more recent study, for the period 1966-1976, also found higher rates among Oxford University students than the general population of similar age, although the difference was far less marked (Hawton, Crowle, Simkin, & Bancroft, 1978). Bearing in mind the small numbers of actual student suicides involved, the rate for male students of 10 per 100,000 and that for females of 13 per 100,000 contrasted with rates of 5.1 and 2.6 among males and females aged 15 to 24 in the general population at the midpoint of the survey period. The authors suggested the possibilities that the relative lowering of the student suicide rates compared with the earlier study may have been related to the advent of student counseling services and the reduction in the student male to female ratio—the former high ratio was thought to be implicated in the suicide problem of male students in Oxford and Cambridge (Cresswell & Smith, 1968).

The British findings have mostly not been substantiated in North America, with, for example, much lower rates of suicide being found in the United States both among students at Yale and Harvard, compared with their British counterparts (Eisenberg, 1980; Parrish, 1957), and in other universities compared with the general population of the same age (Petzel & Cline, 1978). Furthermore, a lower rate of suicide was found among students at Alberta University in Canada than expected from general population figures (Sims & Ball, 1973). It is difficult to explain these transatlantic differences, except to postulate that there might have been, especially in the postwar years, severe stresses on Oxbridge students, and, possibly, a selection policy that tended to allow entry to students at risk of psychological instability into an environment in which many individuals have felt very isolated.

Season of the Year

Among adults there are seasonal fluctuations in the incidence of suicide, with the greatest number of suicides occurring in the spring

(Meares, Mendelsohn, & Milgrom-Friedman, 1981). The same pattern has not been consistently reported for adolescents and children, perhaps because the numbers of cases are too small to reveal seasonal variations. In fact, Garfinkel and Golombek (1983) reported a higher rate of suicide in the autumn and winter among young persons in Ontario. In reviewing the suicide figures for 8 to 17 year olds between 1938 and 1953 in England and Wales, Mulcock (1955) confirmed that there was an excess number of suicides in spring but did not provide statistical evidence for this.

METHODS USED IN SUICIDES

There are considerable international differences in the methods used in suicides by the young. In some countries there have also been changes in these with time.

In North America, firearms are the predominant means of suicide. This presumably reflects their ready availability. There is also some evidence that their use for suicide is increasing (Frederick, 1978). The methods used in the United States in child and adolescent suicides in 1981 are summarized in Table 2.3. Guns were by far the most popular method of committing suicide, especially among 15 to 24 year olds. They were also used in approximately half the suicides of 10 to 14 year olds. A third of the suicidal deaths in this age group were by hanging. As usually found elsewhere, boys were more likely than girls to use violent methods, and girls were more likely to use poisons. Overall, however, poisons (that is, drugs) were little used by both age groups.

Similar patterns of methods of suicide in the young have been reported from Canada, with far more boys than girls using firearms, although there has been some suggestion of an increasing use of violent methods by females. Garfinkel and Golombek (1983) also noticed that firearms were more commonly used for suicide in rural areas of Ontario, whereas drugs and jumping from heights were most common in urban areas, presumably reflecting the differences in accessibility to these methods in the different areas.

In an early British survey of 357 suicides aged under 17, Mulcock (1955) found that, of the boys, half had used hanging or self-strangulation, while a third had poisoned themselves with coal gas. Of

TABLE 2.3

Methods Used in Suicides by Children and Adolescents in the United States (1981)[1] and in England and Wales (1983)[2]

| | Age Groups (Years) | | |
	10-14 United States (percentages)	15-19 United States (percentages)	England & Wales (percentages)
Firearms	52.9	66.0	5.9
Hanging, strangling, and suffocation	32.0	18.0	29.4
Poisoning by liquids and solids	12.8	2.2	23.5
Poisoning by gas	0.6	7.8	5.9
Other	1.7	5.9	35.3*

SOURCES: (1) National Center for Health Statistics (1984) and (2) Office of Population Censuses and Surveys (personal communication). British Crown Copyright; reproduced with the permission of the Controller of Her Majesty's Stationery Office.
NOTE: The figures for 10 to 14 year olds in England and Wales were omitted because of small numbers.
*Jumping from high places was common among the "other" methods in England and Wales.

the girls, on the other hand, almost three-quarters had used coal gas, whereas none had hanged or strangled herself. Among both sexes, the proportion using drug overdoses was extremely small (although, as noted below, this may have reflected failure to identify poisoning deaths as suicide). In attempting to explain the marked preference of boys for strangulation or hanging, Mulcock examined the statistics for accidental death in this age group. He found that, among accidental deaths from strangulation or hanging, boys outnumbered girls by a ratio of over 100 to 1. From this finding he concluded that boys were more likely than girls to experiment with ropes, and other hardware, and thus more likely to choose these methods in committing suicide.

A similar sex pattern was found by Shaffer (1974) in a careful study of 30 British suicidal deaths by under 15 year olds (21 boys and 9 girls). Five boys, but no girls, were found to have chosen hanging as the method of suicide. Overall, however, compared with Mulcock's findings, hanging had been supplanted by carbon monoxide poisoning as the most popular means of death. A small proportion of children (10%) had killed themselves with firearms; all these children lived in rural areas, where guns were more easily available. Three children (10%) used well-planned mechanical methods of committing suicide, such as electrocution and decapitation on a railway line: They were all boys, and all appeared to be of superior intelligence. Shaffer attempted to determine the lethality of the method of suicide by estimating the rapidity with which death might have been expected to occur, and the precautions that the child took to avoid discovery. Using these two criteria, it was possible to decide whether lethality was high or low in 21 cases: Fifteen had used highly lethal methods; of these cases 14 were boys and only one a girl.

In Britain during the 1960s the gas supply was gradually detoxified. Between 1971 and 1980 there were no suicides by domestic gas poisoning among 10 to 14 year olds and only a few by 15 to 19 year olds. There has, however, been a steady increase in the number of suicides by poisoning using liquids or solids (mostly drug overdose) over the past three decades. For example, McClure (1984) reported that among 10 to 14 year olds in England and Wales between 1951 and 1961 there was only one case, whereas there were 26 between 1971 and 1980. Among 15 to 19 year olds there was a more than ninefold increase in the use of poisons and liquids for suicide between 1950 and 1980. The recent situation regarding methods used in suicides by young people in the United Kingdom is shown in Table 2.3.

There has also been a marked increase in recent years in the numbers of deaths due to poisoning by solids or liquids that have received a coroner's verdict of undetermined or accidental death. Because of the doubts surrounding these groups, with the strong possibility that many of these are in fact suicides (Adelstein & Mardon, 1975), and the lesser likelihood of uncertainty that tends to surround deaths when more violent methods have been employed, one wonders whether the recent marked increase in suicidal deaths among teenagers in the United States has not been largely paralleled in Britain, but been disguised because of the differences in the methods commonly used for suicide and hence differences in their likelihood of official identification as suicides.

Interestingly, sex differences in the choice of method for suicide are by no means universally reported. For example, Sathyavathi (1975) found no difference in the proportions of boys and girls using violent methods among 45 Indian suicides of under 15 year olds that were notified to the Bangalore police during a six-year period. Overall, burning and drowning were the most common methods of suicide, each accounting for 38% of cases, hanging was rare, accounting for only 9% of cases. Two interesting findings in this study were that active methods of suicide (for example, burning or hanging) and passive methods of suicide (poisoning and drowning, for instance) were used equally frequently in this sample of young people, and that active methods were used far more commonly than among suicides in the general population.

The findings of this Indian study suggest that psychodynamic interpretations of boys' predilection for violent methods of suicide (for instance, that they are exhibiting a higher aggressive drive than girls) may have only limited application. The findings of a recent study from Singapore suggested that children tend to use whatever methods of suicide are readily available (Chia, 1979). For example, jumping from high-rise flats was the commonest cause of death, followed by hanging (more frequent among boys than girls) and poisoning (more frequent among girls); insecticides were the most commonly ingested poisons. It is possible that, among boys, firearms, ropes, and so on are the most readily available means of suicide, because boys are more used to playing with or handling such objects. Compared with girls, they may be more able to assess their properties, and thus be more likely to use them if they decide to kill themselves.

CONCLUSIONS

Several serious problems are encountered when one examines suicide statistics, especially in young people. It is likely that underreporting of suicidal deaths is particularly common in the young. Nevertheless, there is clear evidence that a very marked increase in suicides by older teenagers occurred during the past three decades in many parts of the Western world. Suicidal deaths are far less common among children and adolescents under the age of 15, but in some countries, especially the United States, these have also increased somewhat. There are racial differences in suicide rates, with blacks in the United States having significantly lower rates than whites. Suicide rates are also high among married teenagers. Surprisingly little information is available concerning the effect of unemployment on suicide rates in young people. There is conflicting evidence concerning suicide rates among students in the United States and Britain, but an increased risk of student suicides has consistently been found in Britain at Oxford and Cambridge Universities.

There are marked international variations in the methods used for suicide, with deaths resulting from the use of firearms being especially common among young people in the United States and, particularly of late, deaths by poisoning being common elsewhere. Such differences, and changes with time, probably reflect variable availability of the different methods.

3

CAUSES OF SUICIDE

While there is a substantial literature concerning the causes of attempted suicide among children and adolescents (Chapter 6), this is not the case for successful suicide. The usual method of studying causes of suicide is through a "psychological postmortem," in which information used to establish a profile of the dead person is gathered from several sources about the individual's background and the events leading up to the suicide. Data on a number of individuals are then used to identify typical features of persons who commit suicide and to delineate subgroups (see Barraclough, Bunch, Nelson, & Sainsbury, 1974; Robins, 1981). There have been very few such studies of young people who have committed suicide, possibly because of the distress that this type of inquiry may cause to the investigator, the fear of distressing relatives and friends of the deceased, and the methodological difficulties that are involved. Before considering possible causes of suicide in the young, the methodological problems involved in this type of investigation will be discussed. An important question concerning causality is why suicide among young people, especially older adolescents, has increased in recent years. This is explored in the final section of this chapter.

METHODOLOGICAL PROBLEMS
IN STUDYING CAUSES

The first problem encountered in attempting to study the causes of suicide results from the necessarily retrospective nature of such an investigation. Information has to be gleaned months or years after the suicide has occurred and may therefore be inadequate; for example, aspects of the child's character, feelings, or educational ability may have gone unrecorded. Furthermore, the information may be inaccurate, in that the recollection of informants may be distorted by the passage of time and by the knowledge that the young person has committed suicide.

A second problem is the difficulty of using parents or siblings as informants. To get accurate and detailed information about the dead person it is obviously important to interview family members. However, it is likely to be extremely distressing for parents to answer questions about their dead son or daughter. They may, for example, be suffering from a heavy burden of guilt, which may render them unwilling to remember certain aspects of the dead child's history or family relationships.

The reluctance to obtain information from relatives means that data about young suicides must be elicited mainly from records held by various institutions, such as school authorities, family doctors, and social or public health agencies. This presents a third problem for the researcher, as these records may be lacking the sort of detail required for any comprehensive study of a young person's character traits, educational ability, worries and preoccupations, interpersonal relationships, or psychiatric symptoms.

Any attempt to examine the relationship between suicide and psychiatric illness is hindered by a fourth methodological problem, in that, compared with adults, psychiatric illness in children and adolescents may be atypical. For example, depression in adolescence may be present as a behavioral disorder without the obvious features such as low mood, sleep disturbance, and loss of concentration found in adult depressive illnesses (Cantwell & Carlson, 1979; Toolan, 1962). Thus, in retrospective investigations, estimating the extent to which psychiatric illness has contributed to suicide is largely a matter of guesswork.

Those factors that *may* have a causal relationship with suicide among children and adolescents are discussed below. However, for the reasons mentioned above, the inferences drawn from research findings must be tentative. In considering contributory factors it is convenient to divide them into two main groups: *background factors* and *problems immediately preceding suicide*.

BACKGROUND FACTORS

In order to find factors that may have causal significance in the backgrounds of people who kill themselves, ideally one should compare suicides with nonsuicides and thereby identify distinguishing characteristics. Such studies are lacking for suicide by young people. Instead, investigators have tried to identify factors that suicides share in common or which on clinical grounds appear to occur unusually often. Although these factors will be considered individually, the readers should be aware that suicide usually results from a constellation of factors, rather than one specific cause.

Family Background

Broken Homes

It is well established that adults who kill themselves often come from broken homes. For example, Dorpat, Jackson, and Ripley (1965) found that 50% of a series of 115 adult suicides were from broken homes, a figure far in excess of that found in the general population at the time of the study. Death of at least one parent during childhood was especially common.

Although the findings are somewhat conflicting, studies of successful suicide in young people suggest that a high proportion come from either broken homes or unhappy families. For example, in a British study of 30 individuals who had committed suicide between the ages of 12 and 14, Shaffer (1974) found that seven had broken homes at the time of their death, and in six further cases the parents had separated by the time of the survey (one to four years after the suicide). By contrast, in an American study of ten adolescent suicides between the ages of 11 and 19, all were living with their natural parents at the time of death, although it is unclear how many were living with one parent only. Eight of the adolescents were said to come from "unhappy families" (Sanborn et al., 1973). However, approximately half of a large number of young suicides in Sacramento County, California, had experienced "loss or family disruption," although the authors did not report how recently these events had occurred prior to the suicide (Cosand, Bourque, & Kraus, 1982).

In spite of the contradictions between the findings of these studies, the weight of evidence suggests that family disruption, by death, separation, or divorce, is common among young suicides. It has also been suggested by McAnarney (1979) that loosening or breaking of family ties may be an important determinant of the varying prevalence of suicide among young people in different societies. In support of this hypothesis, she compared the suicide rates in a number of different geographical areas, such as Seattle, Edinburgh, a Shoshonean Indian reservation, Denmark, and North Sudan. On the basis of this comparison she suggested that the prevalence of suicide was related to the degree of geographical mobility and family disruption found in these societies. For example, the lowest suicide rate was found in North Sudan (1 per 100,000), where there was a structure of close Moslem family units; on the other hand, the highest suicide rate was found in the Indian reservation (98 per 100,000) where there was a lack of family stability. Half the suicides on this reservation were less than 25 years old and, when this group was compared with an age-matched control group, it was found that a higher proportion had had more than one caretaker in childhood (70% compared with 15% of controls), and a much higher proportion had suffered two or more losses by desertion or divorce (50% compared with 10% of controls).

Family History of Psychiatric Disorder and Suicidal Behavior

Psychiatric disorder within the family may be an important contributory factor in suicide. In Shaffer's (1974) study, 55% of the 30 cases had a family history of psychiatric consultation with either a psychiatrist or a general practitioner, and nine parents were heavy drinkers. Psychiatric disorder in family members might contribute to a young person's suicide in any one of several ways. First, there may be a genetic predisposition to depression or other serious mental disorders, which are common among suicides. Second, living with depressed relatives may mean that the young person lacks affection and feels rejected. Psychiatric disorder might also cause irritability and aggression between family members, thereby enhancing this sense of rejection. Third, a depressive disorder in a parent or older sibling might serve as a model for the individual, encouraging the adoption of a morbid or hopeless attitude. Finally, a child or adolescent may find it intolerable living with a parent or sibling with a major psychiatric disorder, especially if the disorder is of psychotic magnitude. This last example occurred in three of Shaffer's subjects.

Suicidal behavior by relatives may also be an important background factor in some suicidal deaths of young people. In Shaffer's study, four first-degree relatives had made suicide attempts before the suicides of the adolescents (and three made subsequent attempts). This proportion with a family history of attempts (13%) is roughly comparable with those found in studies of the families of young people who make nonfatal suicide attempts. Garfinkel and Golombek (1983), for example, reported a figure of 8.3%. The fact that suicidal behavior by members of the families of adolescent suicides is relatively common might reflect the high incidence of psychiatric disorder, especially depression, in these families. However, such behavior may be important in another respect, especially in providing a model of coping behavior for the adolescent. This is considered later in more detail.

Psychiatric Disorders

In spite of the difficulties of retrospectively identifying psychiatric illness in young people, especially children, most studies of completed suicide in this age group suggest a fairly high prevalence of such disorders. For example, in Shaffer's (United Kingdom) study, nine out of the 30 adolescents had been seeing a psychiatrist or were on the waiting list for a psychiatric appointment; only two of these subjects had been referred because of a previous suicide attempt. Six further adolescents were recognized by school authorities as having conduct or emotional problems and had been seen by probation or welfare services. Thus, for half the sample there was evidence of some sort of psychiatric disturbance. When Shaffer tried to identify individual psychiatric symptoms in these children, he found that 22 had *antisocial* symptoms, such as bullying, stealing, or truancy, while 21 had *emotional* symptoms, such as depression, excessive fears, or school refusal; 17 children had symptoms in both categories.

Similar levels of psychological disorder were found in two North American studies. In their study in Sacramento County, California, Cosand and associates (1982) reported that just over a third of 15-19-year-old suicides had shown evidence of "emotional instability," the figure for 20 to 24 year olds being approximately 50%. Of the 15 to 19 year olds, 17% had received psychiatric treatment; again, the proportion of 20 to 24 year olds for whom this was so was somewhat higher. In their study of 10 to 24 year olds in Ontario, Garfinkel and Golombek (1983) noted that "significant psychiatric conditions" were recorded at the time of the inquest or necropsy in a quarter of the cases. Depression was the most common disorder, but 19% of those with psychiatric conditions had been receiving treatment for schizophrenia.

In Singapore, Chia (1979) based his assessment of psychiatric disorder on information in the Singapore coroner's case files, which may have been less complete than, for example, the school, medical, and psychiatric records that were consulted in Shaffer's study. Nevertheless, he considered that psychiatric disorder was the "dominant causal factor" in the death of 32 (23%) of his 137 subjects. Of these 32 adolescents, 24 were considered to be suffering from psychotic illnesses (which, presumably, included depression), four from personality disorders, three from psychosomatic illnesses, and one from acute alcoholism. A rather lower prevalence of mental illness was suggested by Sathyavathi (1975) on the basis of information in the Bangalore police records. Mental illness was identified in 12% of her sample, although no further details were given.

These estimates of the prevalence of psychiatric disorder are somewhat greater than those found in populations of adolescent suicide attempters, but far lower than reported for adult suicides. For example, Barraclough and associates (1974) identified psychiatric disorders in 93% of adult suicides, the vast majority suffering from depression. Although the difficulty in diagnosing psychiatric disorders in young people may contribute to this discrepancy, it seems likely that suicide in the young is more often a reaction to external circumstances and that suicide in adults more often due to hopelessness and despair arising out of severe psychiatric disturbance.

Physical Disorders

Although several studies have suggested that a disproportionate number of adolescent suicide attempters have problems with their physical health, contradictory findings have emerged from studies of completed suicide. Sathyavathi (1975), for example, found that 29% of her series had some sort of physical illness (such as asthma, fits, tonsillitis), although these usually seemed to be less important than social problems. She postulated that the physical illness constituted a predisposing factor that rendered the child more vulnerable to distress caused by social problems, such as punishment by parents, school failure, and the like.

Other studies of young suicides, however, have reported a smaller proportion with physical illnesses. For example, in a study of 137 suicides under the age of 20 in Singapore, Chia (1979) found that physical illness was a "dominant causative factor" in only nine, although it is unclear in what additional proportion it may have been a contributory rather than a dominant causal factor. Physical illness was found in only 3% to 5% of Garfinkel and Golombek's (1983) cases in Ontario. Cosand and associates (1982) reported interesting age differences in this respect; none of their 10 to 14 year olds had physical disorders, whereas such conditions occurred quite often among 15 to 19 year olds and were common in 20 to 24 year olds.

Shaffer (1974) found that only 2 of his 30 adolescents had chronic illnesses. However, he noted an interesting physical abnormality in that a disproportionate number of subjects for whom a record of height was available were tall or very tall for their age.

In summary, it seems likely that although physical illness is important in adult suicides, especially the elderly, it is only rarely a major contributory factor in adolescent and child suicide.

Previous Suicide Attempts

The important overlap between completed suicide and attempted suicide was noted in the first chapter. Many young people who kill themselves have made previous attempts. Shaffer (1974) reported that 46% of his young suicides had previously discussed, threatened, or attempted suicide, eight within 24 hours of their death. Unfortunately, he did not distinguish between previous attempts and discussed or threatened suicide, although a figure of 40% for previous attempts was mentioned in a later report (Shaffer & Fisher, 1981). A similar figure was reported by Cosand and associates (1982). In addition, they found that previous attempts were more common among females than males, perhaps reflecting both the higher incidence of attempted suicide among females in general and the difference in the methods predominantly used by the two sexes, with violent methods more commonly used by males, and drug overdoses, which have a lower likelihood of success, being used more by females.

Intellectual Level

There has been very little investigation of the intelligence of children and adolescents who commit suicide. The only study in which intellectual performance was examined appears to be Shaffer's (1974). Estimates of I.Q. were available for 28 of the 30 cases. These revealed an excess of adolescents with an above-average I.Q. For example, 14 of the 30 had an I.Q. of 115 or more and five had an I.Q. above 130. This is difficult to explain. One possibility is that the appraisal of the hopelessness of a situation by young people, and the planning of a fatal attempt, may require considerable intellectual ability.

Religion

On the basis of the low suicide rates in Catholic countries and among orthodox Jewish communities, McAnarney (1979) suggested that religious culture may influence the suicide rate. With the exception of Sathyavathi's Indian study, in which 93% of the subjects were found to be Hindus, 4% Muslims, and 2% Christians (Sathyavathi, 1975), there has been little research into religious beliefs among young suicides.

PROBLEMS IMMEDIATELY PRECEDING SUICIDE

Although it is useful to separate background, predisposing causal factors from more immediate, precipitating factors, most studies have not made this distinction. However, it is possible to get an impression from the literature of the sorts of problems that may immediately precede suicide in young people.

For example, on the basis of coroners' records of the suicides of thirty 10 to 14 year olds, Shaffer found that a "disciplinary crisis" was the most common problem, occurring in 36% (11) of the sample. In five cases the children had been told by a teacher that their parents were about to be informed of truanting or other antisocial behavior, and in the other six the child was anticipating either punishment at school or court action. Other common problems included fights with peers (13%), disputes with boyfriends or girlfriends (10%), disputes with parents (10%), and interaction with a psychotic parent (10%). The three adolescents who had a problem with a psychotic parent were a particularly interesting group as they had each expressed distress at having to live with a mad parent. Two of these teenagers killed themselves on the day that a psychotic parent was due to be discharged from a psychiatric hospital.

A surprising finding was that seven of the 30 adolescents in Shaffer's study died within two weeks of their birthdays; this was three times the proportion that was expected by chance. In a further six cases, bereavement was mentioned at the inquest as a possible contributory factor; for two individuals the loss involved parents and for four it involved grandparents. However, there appeared to be no relationship between the anniversary of the bereavement and the date of the suicide.

In her Bangalore study, Sathyavathi (1975) reported that, of the 35 adolescents for whom information was available, 43% had social problems, such as punishment by parents, ill-treatment, or fear of examinations, although it is unclear whether these were chronic difficulties or acute precipitants. A similar difficulty in separating chronic from acute difficulties arises in evaluating the findings of Chia's (1979) Singapore study. The author considered that social problems were the "dominant causal factor" in 40 of the 137 cases, while interpersonal problems were the dominant factor in 56 cases. The most common social problems involved work, national service, school and examinations. The most common interpersonal difficulties were being reprimanded, love problems, and marital problems.

The precipitants for suicide by young people are obviously likely to vary according to the individual's social environment and what is construed as particularly stressful or threatening. In Japan, for example, which has extremely high suicide rates among the young, it has been argued by Igu (1981) that the intensely stressful preparation for the college entrance examination, the outcome of which virtually decides the individual's future, is a major factor in such suicides.

WHY HAS SUICIDE BECOME
MORE COMMON AMONG YOUNG PEOPLE?

Evidence reported in the previous chapter demonstrated conclusively that a substantial increase in suicide by young people, especially older teenagers, occurred during the past two or more decades. Clearly one must try to explain this phenomenon, although it must be emphasized that attempts to do so rest almost entirely on hypotheses that cannot be tested. The following are some tentative explanations. They are by no means exclusive, each possibly having a role in this phenomenon and all likely to be interrelated.

Changes in the Social Environment

There is no doubt that the social environment of young people in the West has undergone vast changes during the past three decades. One change has been a reduction in family ties, particularly as a result of the increasing divorce rate. Loss of family supports is becoming more common and often occurs at an early age. This has coincided with a trend for young people to face pressure associated with adulthood earlier in life. For example, sexual relationships are now often established at a younger age than was true in the past, so that there is a greater likelihood of the young experiencing the disruption of serious relationships. Such stresses are now commonly suffered by young people in the absence of supports. Evidence is accumulating concerning the importance of supportive relationships at such times, and how, if they are lacking, depression is a likely consequence (Brown & Harris, 1978). In view of the well-established link between depression and suicide, this may be one factor contributing to the increase in the suicide rate among the young. Durkheim (1897) was the first to postulate that lack of social integration and social isolation might explain suicide. Although he was primarily concerned with suicide among adults, his theory might also apply to the young.

Greater Acceptability of Suicide as an Option

Changing attitudes among the young toward suicide might be another factor. It is well known that suicide rates tend to be higher in countries such as Japan, where, historically, suicide has been viewed as an acceptable option, compared with other countries, such as those that are predominantly Roman Catholic, in which suicide is regarded as a sin. With the increasing tendency to question the reasons for existence, particularly with the threat of nuclear war, and the weakening of religious faith, it is possible that the inhibitions on suicide may be decreasing, although it is difficult to assemble evidence for this.

A further factor that might have influenced attitudes to suicide is the increasingly free discussion of the topic in the media. There has been concern in the United States that a media-related contagion effect might partly explain the increase in suicides by older teenagers. For example, in Plano, Texas, seven suicides occurred among 15 to 18 year olds between February 19 and August 22, 1983 ("Cluster phenomenon," 1984). There were clear links between some of the suicides. Two of the boys involved were friends. Another dead boy was found to have newspaper clippings concerning two of the suicides pinned up in his room. In Westchester County, New York, five young suicides occurred during less than three weeks at the beginning of 1984 ("Cluster phenomenon," 1984). None of these victims knew one another, but the events, starting with the second suicide, received much attention in the local media. There is, of course, the possibility that such clusters occur purely by chance on the basis of random fluctuations. However, the connections between some of the cases in the Plano cluster render this explanation unlikely. Furthermore, there is earlier evidence that media publicity concerning suicides may contribute to such clustering (Bollen & Phillips, 1982; Phillips, 1974). The increase in suicides in California following the death of Marilyn Monroe is particularly well known. In the south of England, Barraclough and colleagues (1977) demonstrated a clear statistical association between reports of suicide in a local newspaper and the subsequent suicide of men under 45 years of age. Several other studies concerning the possible facilitatory influence of publicity on suicides have been reported. In view of the particularly extensive publicity of deaths among the young, this factor might operate most powerfully in this age group.

What might be the mechanisms in such a phenomenon? One possibility is that there is a direct ripple effect, with imitation being the major factor. A more likely explanation is that people who have entertained suicidal ideas, which are common among young people, but who would not normally have carried out a suicidal act, may be encouraged to act on these ideas because of the media reports. This has important implications for prevention, which will be discussed in a later chapter.

Increased Use of Medication and Drugs

During the past two decades there has been such an enormous increase in the use of mood-altering medication that tranquilizers and antidepressants have come to be accepted as a means of dealing with dysphoria, even if this is the direct result of stress rather than psychiatric disorder (Trethowan, 1975). This has been paralleled by a vast increase in deliberate self-poisoning by young people. A connection between the two phenomena is likely (Chapter 5). Increased prescribing of psychotropic medicines might contribute to an increase in suicide because of the resulting relatively low thresholds to taking drugs to deal with stress. This might lead to greater acceptance of self-poisoning as a means of coping, and the consequent increased risk of suicide resulting from overdoses in which death was not the intended outcome, as well as an increase in intended suicidal deaths. However, such an explanation must take account of the fact that the sex ratio in completed suicide is the opposite of that in attempted suicide (although the difference is not so marked for deaths by poisoning), and that, at least in the United Kingdom, there was an actual decline in the rates of official suicide verdicts among the young during the late 1960s and early 1970s, the very time when attempted suicide by self-poisoning was showing the greatest increase.

Drug abuse among the young has also become very much more common in recent years. This has almost certainly contributed to the increase in suicidal deaths, probably because of two factors. The first is that drug addiction often leads to social disintegration and depression. The second is that deaths from overdoses involving illicit drugs are common—whether these should actually be classified as suicidal or accidental is open to question, although the risk of life involved in such behavior is often well recognized by the addicts themselves.

CONCLUSIONS

The likely causes of suicide in children and adolescents are many, the behavior usually resulting from a complex interaction of factors, some being related to the individual's background and others to more immediate events. The investigator who attempts to unravel the causes faces a very difficult task, partly because there may not be adequate access to important information. Nevertheless, it is often apparent that there has been major disruption in the young suicide's background, through death or separation of parents, so that important family supports may be lacking. Other authors have suggested that, even in an intact family structure, the suicidal youth may have been rejected by the parents, with a similar reduction in support. When faced by an acute stress, such as the break-up of an important relationship or a disciplinary crisis, the young person, feeling abandoned, may contemplate suicide as an acceptable option. Depression, especially if it leads to a sense of hopelessness, may increase the likelihood of the person initiating a suicidal act.

Some authors have stressed psychological explanations of suicide by the young (see Zilboorg, 1936), while others have laid greater emphasis on social explanations (e.g., Durkheim, 1897). However, an integration of these two approaches would seem to be the most fruitful. Thus, individuals should be considered in terms of early experiences that have influenced their views of themselves and of their existence, the extent to which they feel supports are to hand at times of stress, and the nature of the stresses they face. Psychiatric disorder, which may be both a cause and a consequence of disturbed social relationships and diminished self-esteem, must be accommodated in any such model, at least in a substantial proportion of individuals, although probably less often than when explaining adult suicides.

In order to explain the increasing numbers of suicides by young people, one must look for evidence of changes in any of the factors mentioned above, plus any new developments. Undeniably, broken homes and consequent loss of family supports have become more common. Attitudes to suicide may also have changed. Media reporting of suicidal deaths may occasionally encourage other young people who are entertaining suicidal ideas to act on these. Finally, increased use of medication to allay distress, and escalation in the rates of deliberate self-poisoning and drug addiction, may be additional factors.

4

AFTERMATH OF CHILD AND ADOLESCENT SUICIDE

There is little doubt that suicidal deaths cause greater difficulties for survivors than most other forms of death, and that the stresses imposed on family members by suicide of a child or adolescent are especially severe. In this chapter the immediate and longer-term effects of suicide on survivors will be examined, and then what little information is available about counseling such individuals will be reviewed.

REACTIONS TO SUICIDE

The reactions of family members who have experienced a suicide are likely to be complex (Worden, 1983), but typically include the following:

(1) *Denial*, including refusal to accept the fact of death, or that it was due to suicide.
(2) *Anger*, which may be directed toward the deceased, as well as toward medical agencies, friends of the deceased, the coroner, and others.
(3) *Shame*, because of the stigma associated with suicide.
(4) *Guilt*, about what the survivor might or should have done to prevent the suicide, as well as about how he or she may have contributed to it.
(5) *Fear*, about the individual's own self-destructive impulses.

Further special factors may add to the stress faced by parents when the suicide is that of a child or adolescent. For example, the stigma and guilt they feel may be extreme. Unfortunately, there is little information on this matter, and even less about how to help survivors of suicide by young people. In part this is the result of the rarity of such suicides by comparison with adult suicides, but also reflects both the unwillingness of many families to be investigated after a suicide, and the reluctance of research workers to tackle such a difficult and painful task. However, there have been a few investigations in the United States that have helped illuminate this important topic, and that are considered below.

How Society Reacts to Suicide by Young People

Some investigators have examined the question of whether particular stigma results from the suicide of a young person when compared with death from other causes. For example, Calhoun, Selby, and Faulstich (1980) used four newspaper reports of deaths of 10 year olds, two reporting suicides by first a boy and then by a girl, and two reporting deaths of a boy and a girl from physical illness, to explore the attitudes of members of the general public to such deaths. The parents of the children who died by suicide were judged to be emotionally disturbed, were less liked (especially the fathers), and were blamed more than the parents of children who died from natural causes. The sex of the child did not affect the attitudes of the respondents to the parents.

The more negative attitudes toward parents of a young child who had died by suicide as compared with attitudes toward parents of a child who died from natural causes were confirmed in a later study using a similar "projective" technique (Calhoun et al., 1982). In addition, it appeared that extenuating factors that might mitigate negative judgments toward parents in other types of death did not appear to affect their attitudes when the death was suicide.

A similar method of investigation was used by Rudestam and Imbroll (1983), but they also included a newspaper report of a death of a child in an automobile accident, and used two reports of deaths by suicide, one involving a violent suicide (by hanging) and the other a nonviolent suicide (barbiturate overdose). This study confirmed that parents of child suicides are perceived more negatively than parents of children who die from natural causes, but also suggested that children who use violent means for suicide are regarded as coming from more disturbed home environments than those who use nonviolent means. No differences in attitudes were found between respondents who were themselves parents and those who were not. However, and perhaps somewhat surprisingly, those respondents who knew someone who had committed suicide felt more anger toward the parents of the child suicides in the newspaper reports than those who had not been acquainted with people who had killed themselves. Rudestam and Imbroll commented, "To the extent that children's suicidal behaviour reflects motives of punishment and revenge directed at unresponsive parents, their actions may, from one perspective, be deemed successful."

Reactions and Experiences of Families of Young Suicides

Thus far, only indirect studies using newspaper reports have been considered. What about the actual reactions and experiences of families who have experienced the loss of a child or adolescent through suicide?

The typical reactions to suicide listed at the beginning of this chapter have been confirmed in three studies of small numbers of parents of young suicides (Hatton & Valente, 1981; Herzog & Resnik, 1967; Rudestam, 1977). The immediate shock and distress on hearing the news of the death often appeared to affect one parent more than the other. Denial and hostility were especially common among fathers, who in particular tended to attribute blame to factors outside the family, such as friends of the deceased, school pressure, availability of drugs, and the permissiveness of society (Rudestam, 1977). The tendency to explain the death as an accident rather than suicide was common, and indeed Herzog and Resnik (1967) were often asked if they could arrange falsification of the death certification.

Guilt was a universal finding. This is not surprising as parents assume responsibility for the development of their children, and the fact of a child taking his or her own life represents a supreme denigration of the parents' capabilities. The fact that families of young people who died by suicide may display many other problems, such as abuse, violence, and alcoholism, is likely to exacerbate the distress of family members, including their guilt. Some parents had experienced chronic distress and aggravation in coping with their children, and occasionally there was a sense of relief when the suicide occurred. However, this in turn tended to fuel their feelings of guilt.

The negative attitudes of society toward parents of young suicides were confirmed when the parents themselves were interviewed. Hatton and Valente (1981) suggested that the parents' mourning was prohibited by their social network, friends avoiding discussion of the death, or even avoiding the parents altogether. Further inhibition of mourning resulted from blocked communication between the parents and other family members and between the parents themselves. Previous important sources of support therefore became unavailable. Fathers in particular tended to suffer in a very private and introspective fashion. Attempts to share personal distress with the spouse were often avoided because of fear of burdening or upsetting that person. Rudestam (1977) noted that there seemed to be an implicit agreement between some parents not to discuss the death and this seemed to be a major factor that prevented progress in the grieving process.

Further important consequences of suicide of a child or adolescent may involve other children in the family. Hatton and Valente (1981) noted that the death of a child is likely to invalidate a parent's sense of parental identity and to disturb his or her ability to exert appropriate control within the family. Decisions concerning discipline may prove especially difficult, with a tendency to be either overpermissive or overstrict. This may stem partly from a fear that another child in the family might resort to suicide.

Unfortunately, little appears to be known about the reactions of young siblings to suicide of a brother or sister. Parents who have had a son or daughter die by suicide are likely to refuse to allow other young children to be interviewed about the event and their feelings concerning the loss (Herzog & Resnik, 1967).

COUNSELING THE SURVIVORS OF CHILD AND ADOLESCENT SUICIDE

Far more is known about helping the survivors of adult suicide (Worden, 1983) than those of child and adolescent suicide, presumably in part at least because of the very different rates of occurrence of suicide in the two age groups. It seems likely, however, that many of the principles inherent in counseling relatives and friends of suicides are common to both, although there will be some special further requirements for the families of young suicides.

Worden (1983) emphasized the use of the following strategies during suicide counseling:

(1) Helping establish accurate communication between family members.

(2) Reality testing feelings of guilt. For example, people may be helped to see that they had done all they could for the deceased. Sometimes there is good reason for guilt, which may pose great difficulty for the counselor. The bereaved person will need assistance in accepting the feelings of guilt and preventing them becoming distorted.

(3) Correcting distortions, so that the deceased is viewed realistically, rather than as all good or all bad.

(4) Exploring attitudes toward the future, in order to help survivors see how the death will affect them in the long term.

(5) Encouraging ventilation of anger, and giving a person permission to have such feelings.

(6) Exploring the survivors' sense of abandonment.

On the basis of their study of parents who had lost children through suicide, Herzog and Resnik (1967) made the following recommendations about counseling. They suggested that a trained professional person should see the parents within 24 hours of the death. This was because several of the parents in their study said they would have appreciated the immediate help of a professionally trained person who could have talked to them about their feelings at the time. Such a person might be from a suicide prevention center or linked to a coroner's office. However, it was most important that the counselor should not be involved in the official investigation of the suicide.

The first visit should be supportive. Later visits should be particularly concerned with exploring feelings of guilt, correcting distorted attitudes toward the deceased, and so on, as suggested above. Herzog and Resnik suggested that these visits could become less frequent by six months after the death, although they did not specify the frequency of visits up until that time. Visits perhaps every two to three weeks would be appropriate in most cases. Later, the visits could occur when the family felt they needed them. However, Herzog and Resnik made the important suggestion that the counselor should arrange a visit around the time of the anniversary of the death, indicating awareness that this may be a difficult time for many suicide survivors because mourning is likely to be reawakened.

Hatton and Valente (1981) have described a group counseling approach that they offered to eight parents of young suicides in Los Angeles. The groups met for ten sessions in all, weekly for the first eight weeks and then fortnightly for the last two. The suicides had occurred between six weeks and six months before the group began. The members of the group seemed somewhat unusual in that there was little evidence of disturbed family relations prior to the suicides. As will be apparent from the previous chapter, this is not true for the majority of young suicides. During the initial meetings of the group there was considerable ventilation and sharing of feelings. In the middle phase of the group's life the group members offered each other support and reassurance, and discussed ways of coping with the loss. The parents felt safe enough to express their feelings of hostility and anger. Discussion often turned to the group members' loss of confidence in their roles as parents and the possible effects of the suicide on their other children.

By the time the group ended, Hatton and Valente thought that the parents were less depressed and more able to plan for the future. They also noted that the fathers, in particular, were now more able to express anger toward the dead child.

CONCLUSIONS

This chapter has focused on the survivors of suicide by young people. Unfortunately, little is known about the difficulties they face although it is obvious that these are considerable. Negative attitudes of friends and other relatives following the suicide may impose a special burden on parents. Previous family pathology may add to the guilt and anger evoked by the death. Parents often feel their role as parents has been severely undermined, and this may make relationships with their other children difficult. Discipline may prove a particular problem. Little is known about the effects of the suicide on the dead individual's siblings.

Counseling for the families of young suicides would seem to be imperative. Although some recommendations for how this might occur have been discussed, this is an area that requires much more attention. Appropriate assistance for family members during the months following the suicide might help prevent the development of severe and chronic psychological problems. It might also alleviate interpersonal difficulties, especially blocked communication, which often interfere with the expression of grief.

5

EPIDEMIOLOGY AND NATURE OF ATTEMPTED SUICIDE

This chapter begins with a discussion of the problems involved in determining the extent of attempted suicide among the young, following which the recent trends in this behavior in different parts of the world are examined. In the subsequent sections the demographic characteristics of young suicide attempters, the methods used in attempts, and the possible "contagious" nature of attempted suicide are explored.

PROBLEMS IN ASCERTAINING THE EXTENT OF ATTEMPTED SUICIDE

Different problems face the investigator examining attempted suicide among children and adolescents from those that were discussed earlier when considering the epidemiology of completed suicide. These include the problems of case definition and identification.

The Problem of Definition

Considerable confusion abounds in the literature because some workers do not distinguish clearly between young people who have suicidal thoughts or make suicidal threats and those who make actual suicide attempts. Suicidal thoughts are very much more common than threats or actual attempts, as exemplified by the fact that in a survey of school children in England, 4.5% of the boys and 9.4% of the girls admitted to having experienced relatively serious suicidal ideation at some time (Bagley, 1975). There are also likely to be important differences between young people who consider or threaten suicide and those who carry out suicidal acts.

A further problem of definition is that some workers have distinguished two categories of suicide attempts on the basis of the apparent intention; thus, the "suicidal gesture" may be distinguished from the "serious suicidal attempt." This distinction is not useful for epidemiological purposes (although it is important when making clinical assessments) because it will necessarily be made on the basis of researchers' subjective judgments. In epidemiological studies it is preferable to define attempted suicide on the basis of behavior alone, rather than on inferences about intention. In several investigations conducted in Oxford, the following definitions of nonfatal suicidal behavior (Bancroft, Skrimshire, Reynolds, Simkin, & Smith, 1975; Hawton & Catalan, 1982) have been found useful and seem to overcome this problem:

- *Deliberate self-poisoning*—the deliberate ingestion of more than the prescribed amount of medicinal substances, or ingestion of substances never intended for human consumption, irrespective of whether harm was intended.
- *Deliberate self-injury*—any intentional self-inflicted injury, irrespective of the apparent purpose of the act.

Case Identification

Some studies of attempted suicide in young persons are based on cases admitted to psychiatric hospitals (e.g. Stanley & Barter, 1970). More usually, cases are identified on the basis of referrals to general hospitals. In one study of attempted suicide in all age groups, Whitehead, Johnson, & Ferrence (1973) tried to identify all overdoses and self-injuries that occurred in a particular community by obtaining information not only on general hospital referrals, but also on suicide attempts in psychiatric hospitals and jails, and those identified by social and other health care agencies and not referred to hospital. The number of cases identified by these means represented an increase of more than

100% over the number identified *only* on the basis of general hospital referral. Clearly the perceived size of the problem of attempted suicide depends to a great extent on the method by which cases are identified.

A further difficulty in case identification that is particularly pertinent when studying children and adolescents is the distinction between accidents and deliberate attempts. There is likely to be greater willingness to accept overdoses and injuries among young people, especially children, as accidental because of reluctance to acknowledge (or lack of awareness of the fact) that suicidal actions occur in this age group. An impressive demonstration of failure to identify suicide attempts by young people was provided by McIntire and Angle (1973) who investigated 50 individuals aged between 6 and 18 years who had been treated at a poison control center in the United States. Whereas the initial hospital diagnoses were "accidents" in 42% and "suicide attempts" in 58%, following a "psychological biopsy," which included careful interview of the subjects and, where possible, one or both of their parents, the proportion in which there was good evidence that a suicidal act had occurred increased to 72%. (Furthermore, only 4% of the diagnoses remained as accidents, 22% now being thought to have been "intoxications" and one case an attempted homicide.)

TRENDS IN ATTEMPTED SUICIDE AMONG YOUNG PEOPLE

It is extremely difficult to obtain statistics concerning attempted suicide. Efforts to do so are hampered by the fact that registries to record such statistics, in the way that mortality statistics are recorded, are lacking. Furthermore, use of general hospital referral statistics is disappointing because, at least in the United Kingdom, suicide attempts are usually not recorded as such in official returns, but instead are classed as "adverse effects of drugs" in the case of overdoses, and according to the nature of the injury in the case of self-injury. As a result, evidence concerning the epidemiology of attempted suicide is only available from studies specifically established to look at this problem. Most of these rely on general hospital statistics, and it has already been noted how these are likely to provide an underestimate of the true extent of the behavior. It will be obvious, therefore, how difficult it is to obtain evidence that allows one to make either national or international comparisons. However, some of the available evidence is considered below.

United States

Surprisingly little information is available concerning trends in nonfatal suicidal behavior in the United States. Although there was an increase in the proportion of under 21 year olds among the total population of attempters referred to the emergency room of the Yale-New Haven Hospital in New Haven between 1970 and 1975 (Wexler, Weissman, & Kasl, 1978), O'Brien (1977) could detect no increase in referrals of teenagers following overdoses to the emergency room of Massachusetts General Hospital in Boston between 1964 and 1974. However, most people who have written on the topic of adolescent attempted suicide in the United States have commented on the recent marked increase in this behavior although statistical evidence has often been lacking.

United Kingdom

Considerable information accrued during the 1960s and 1970s documenting a vast increase in the rates of attempted suicide among young people in the United Kingdom. The increase was most marked for drug overdoses. For example, in the Scottish city of Edinburgh, between 1968-1969 and 1974-1975, Kreitman and Schreiber (1979) detected a 250% increase in the referral rates (based on the Edinburgh population figures) of girls in the 15 to 19 age group following self-poisoning or self-injury. The greatest increase was among girls aged 15 to 17 years. (No findings for under 15 year olds, nor for boys, were reported.) By 1974-1975, an average of more than one out of every hundred girls in the 15 to 19 year age group was referred to hospital following a suicide attempt each year.

In England, general hospital admission statistics for "adverse effects of drugs" were used to study self-poisoning among teenagers in the Oxford region after it was demonstrated that 97.5% of such cases in this age group were actually definite cases of deliberate self-poisoning

(Hawton & Goldacre, 1982). This study revealed evidence of a further increase in attempts by self-poisoning after the mid-1970s, but less marked than had been reported for the 1968-1975 period by Kreitman and Schreiber in Edinburgh. Between 1974 and 1979 there was an overall increase of 28% in the rates of admission for self-poisoning among 12 to 20 year olds. There was, however, evidence of a greater increase among 12 to 15 year olds (35%) than among 16 to 20 year olds (23%). During this period, admissions for self-poisoning accounted for 4.7% of all general hospital admissions among 12 to 20 year olds.

Australasia

An epidemiological study of attempted suicide in Melbourne for the period 1963 to 1970 revealed a severalfold increase in this behavior among 15- to 19-year-old boys, compared with only a 19% increase in the number of boys in this age group in the general population, and a twofold increase in the number of 15 to 19 year old girls making attempts compared with only a 21% increase in the number of girls in this age group in the general population (Oliver, Kaminski, Tudor, & Hetzel, 1971).

Trends in self-poisoning in Hobart, Tasmania, between 1968 and 1972, were reported by Mills, Williams, Sale, Perkin, and Henderson (1974), who noted a 150% increase in rates among 15 to 19 year old girls, and a smaller increase among boys in the same age group. They particularly commented on a very marked increase in the number of secondary schoolgirls who took overdoses during this period.

In general, therefore, it appears that during the later 1960s and early 1970s there was a very marked rise in the incidence of nonfatal suicidal behavior among young people. Since then there has been a further gradual increase in this behavior, but with perhaps a more substantial increase among *young* teenagers. The numbers of attempted suicides far outnumber completed suicides in this age group, particularly among girls. In France, for example, Choquet, Facy, and Davidson (1980) reported a ratio of 160 to 1 for girls, and 25 to 1 for boys in the 15 to 24 age group.

Attempted suicide has now become one of the major health care problems in young people throughout most of the Western world. Why should there have been such a dramatic increase in this behavior, especially drug overdoses, among the young? Greater use of medication to deal with stress, fueled by the increased prescribing of psychotropic drugs, may be one factor. Wider availability of drugs used for kicks may be another. Furthermore, young people may now face greater social pressures, due perhaps partly to earlier expectation of adult behavior, which is not matched by psychological maturity. It also seems likely that fashion has played a part in the increase in self-poisoning, with imitation being a powerful factor.

DEMOGRAPHIC CHARACTERISTICS

Age and Sex

Attempted suicide is relatively rare under the age of 12 years, although suicidal *thoughts* and *threats* are fairly common among children seen in child psychiatry clinics. For example, 13 (33.3%) out of 39 outpatient children aged 6 to 12 years seen at a psychiatric clinic in New York had entertained suicidal ideas, made suicidal threats, or made actual attempts (Pfeffer, Conte, Plutchik, & Jerrett, 1980). However, there were only five (13%) cases in the last category. Lukianowicz (1968) detected these phenomena in approximately 8% of children referred to child guidance clinics in Northern Ireland, with actual attempts in 4% of cases. In a series of 30 cases of attempted suicide in the age range 9 to 15 years in Scotland, five (17%) were aged 9 to 11 years (Haldane & Haider, 1967).

Recently there have been disturbing reports of suicidal behavior by children aged under five years. Rosenthal and Rosenthal (1984), for example, reported 16 such cases who were referred to a child psychiatry outpatient clinic, thirteen of the children having made multiple attempts. Some of the attempts appeared to have been quite serious (such as ingesting drugs, running into fast traffic, and jumping from high places). However, there appears to be no information on how common such behavior is at this age; generally it is thought to be extremely rare, although the risk of an attempt by a young child being unrecognized as such must be very high.

Suicide attempts of children under 12 years of age are more commonly made by boys than girls (Kosky, 1982; Rosenthal &

Rosenthal, 1984). However, after the age of 12, when this behavior becomes increasingly common, the majority of attempters are girls. This is illustrated in Figure 5.1, which shows the age and sex pattern found in a survey of 4232 episodes of self-poisoning among teenagers in the Oxford region between 1974 and 1979 (Hawton & Goldacre, 1982). The rates for girls steadily increased from age 12, reaching a peak at age 16, and then continuing at the same level until age 20. Among boys the rates increased much more slowly, the increase continuing throughout the teenage years. Interestingly, the patterns of self-poisoning with increasing age for the two sexes found in this study were almost exactly replicated in a study in western Australia using the same methodology (Goldacre, personal communication).

In virtually all studies of attempted suicide among teenagers, girls have outnumbered boys, with the ratio usually being in the range 3 to 1 to 9 to 1 (Garfinkel, Froese, & Golombek, 1979; Hawton, O'Grady, Osborn, & Cole, 1982; Otto, 1972; Rohn, Sarles, Kenny, Reynolds, & Head, 1977; Taylor & Stansfield, 1984; Tuckman & Connon, 1962; Walker, 1980; White, 1974). These ratios are different from those found in adults, among whom, although women do outnumber men, the ratio is usually found to be of the order of 1.5 to 1 to 2 to 1 (Wexler et al., 1978). Three possible explanations for the great excess of young female attempters come to mind. The first is that girls may mature and face problems of adulthood, such as broken relationships with boyfriends, earlier than boys. Second, self-poisoning may be a more acceptable coping strategy in girls than boys, the latter only seeming to resort to suicidal behavior in the face of very severe difficulties (Hawton, O'Grady et al., 1982). Third, boys may have alternative outlets for dealing with distress, such as aggressive behavior or heavy alcohol consumption.

A small subgroup of girls who are at special risk of attempted suicide are teenage wives (Bancroft et al., 1975; Kreitman & Schreiber, 1979). Often it appears that these girls may have taken flight from their unhappy families only to end up in disastrous marriages.

Social Class and Education

There are conflicting findings concerning the social class backgrounds of young suicide attempters. In Sweden, Bergstrand and Otto

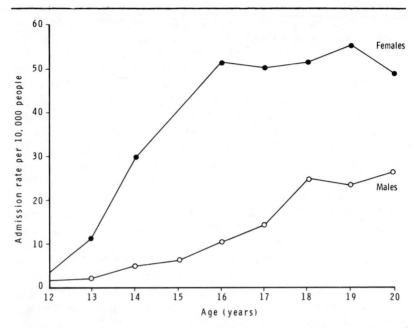

SOURCE: From Hawton and Goldacre (1982). Reproduced by kind permission of the editor of the *British Journal of Psychiatry.*

Figure 5.1   General hospital admissions of adolescents in the Oxford region following deliberate self-poisoning, 1974-1979 (average admission rates per 10,000).

(1962) found an association with lower social class, whereas in two studies in the United Kingdom it appeared that adolescent suicide attempters had a social class distribution similar to that of the general population (White, 1974; Hawton, O'Grady, et al., 1982). However, as we shall see later, it is the family backgrounds of these adolescents that most clearly distinguish them from other young people.

The increased risk of completed suicide among university students was noted earlier (Chapter 2). By contrast, the risk of attempted suicide appears to be decreased among university students. This was demonstrated in a study in Oxford in which the rates of attempted suicide during term-time among students attending the university were compared with the rates among people other than university students in the age group 15 to 24 years, also during term-time, for the academic years 1972-1973 and 1975-1976 (Hawton et al., 1978). As can be seen from

TABLE 5.1

Attempted Suicide Rates per 100,000 for Oxford University
Students and for Age Group 15 to 24 in Oxford City
During University Terms 1972-1973 and 1975-1976[1]

	Male			Female		
University Terms	*Population at Risk*	*N*	*Rate per 100,000 during University Terms*	*Population at Risk*	*N*	*Rate per 100,000 during University Terms*
University students						
1972-1973	8923	7	78	2235	8	358
1975-1976	8858	7	79	2689	3	112
All persons aged 15 to 24 other than university students (Oxford City)						
1972-1973	6255	12	192	6553	46	702
1975-1976	6647	22	331	6631	50	754

SOURCE: Hawton et al. (1978). Reproduced by kind permission of the editor of the *British Journal of Psychiatry.*

University students versus all other persons aged 15 to 24 in Oxford City.
1972-1973 males χ^2 = 5.98, p < .01; females χ^2 = 3.8, p < .10.
1975-1976 males χ^2 = 17.03, p < .001; females χ^2 = 14.87, p < .001.
1. Rates are for equivalent periods for both populations.

Table 5.1, there was clear evidence of a lower attempted suicide rate among the university students of both sexes. This difference may well be explicable in terms of the markedly different social class structure among the students, the majority of whom are from the upper social classes, because among young adults (as opposed to adolescents) far higher rates of attempted suicide are found among those of lower compared with those of higher social class (Holding, Buglass, Duffy, & Kreitman, 1977).

METHODS USED IN ATTEMPTS

Attempted suicide in young people most commonly involves deliberate self-poisoning. In a large series of Swedish cases studied by Otto

(1972), 86.9% involved drug ingestion. However, as in adult attempters, there is some degree of sex difference. Thus females use drug overdoses more often than do male attempters. Males more often use violent means such as jumping, hanging, and shooting (Otto, 1972; Mehr, Zeltzer, & Robinson, 1981), many attempts by males being more dangerous than those by females (Miller, Sakinofsky, & Streiner, 1979).

Deliberate Self-Poisoning

As we shall see later, overdoses by children and adolescents are mostly taken very impulsively, with maybe little more than a few minutes' forethought. Therefore the drugs commonly used are those most readily available, such as analgesics (aspirin) and psychotropic agents (Hawton & Goldacre, 1982). The majority of overdoses in this age group involve relatively little threat to life (Barter, Swaback, & Todd, 1968; Hawton, Cole, O'Grady, & Osborn, 1982). However, this is by no means always so. In the United Kingdom, for example, there has recently been a very large increase in the number of overdoses of paracetamol and paracetamol-containing drugs. This trend has probably been paralleled in the United States (Rumack, 1983), where paracetamol is known as acetaminophen. These overdoses are associated with a significant risk of death due to liver toxicity (Davidson & Eastham, 1966). Gazzard and colleagues (1976) found that most people (many of whom were in the 12 to 20 age group) admitted to a liver unit following paracetamol overdoses did not know of the hepatic effects; nearly all said they would not have taken the drug if they had known that delayed liver damage could have developed. In addition, distalgesic, a commonly available combination of paracetamol and dextropropoxyphene, which is frequently used in overdoses, carries serious risk of respiratory depression and death.

Other types of overdose associated with serious danger to life are those involving drugs taken for "kicks," especially hard drugs. It is often difficult to distinguish between deliberate and mistaken overdoses; in some ways it could be argued that it is artificial to do so since experimentation with drugs often appears to include a lack of concern about survival.

Deliberate Self-Injury

The types of self-injury that occur in attempted suicide can be divided into three broad categories (Hawton & Catalan, 1982):

(1) Superficial Self-Cutting. The cuts are usually made on the wrist or forearm and are mostly associated with little or no suicidal intent. Typically, the cuts are superficial. Repeated self-cutting is common, and appears to be associated with eating disorders and with alcohol and drug abuse. Menstrual disturbances often occur in girls who cut themselves (Rosenthal, Rinzler, & Klausner, 1972; Simpson, 1975). These include negative reactions to the onset of menstruation, dislike of periods, and menstrual irregularity. There is conflicting evidence as to whether cutting is more likely during a specific phase of the menstrual cycle (Simpson, 1976).

As with overdoses, the usual precipitants are actual or threatened loss, or an impasse in a personal relationship (Simpson, 1975). Often the behavior is preceded by feelings of tension, and the cuts may be made when the person feels depersonalized or dissociated. He or she may suddenly become aware of the cut, having experienced no pain. The sight of blood may provide a sense of relief, mingled with feelings of disgust or guilt.

Self-cutting sometimes occurs in an epidemic fashion in adolescent inpatient psychiatric units (Offer & Barglow, 1960; Simpson, 1975). Imitation and competition between the adolescents are likely to be important factors in such epidemics.

(2) Serious Self-Injury. This category includes hanging, jumping from heights, shooting, and jumping in front of vehicles, as well as deep cutting of the throat and neck. These methods are used far more often by boys than by girls, and almost invariably are associated with serious suicidal intent. Because of the difference in availability of firearms, shooting is far more common in the United States than in European countries.

(3) Self-Mutilation. Such acts, which may include, for example, damage to the genitals or to the eyes, are rare in young people. They are

usually the result of serious psychiatric disorder, including schizo-phrenia, in which the mutilation may occur as a consequence of a delusional belief or a hallucinatory command.

CONTAGIOUS ASPECTS OF ATTEMPTED SUICIDE

Suicidal behavior often appears to have an epidemic or contagious nature in the sense that an act by one individual may be linked with that by another, not necessarily because they are facing the same stresses, but because of imitation or competition. This particularly applies to attempted suicide among children and adolescents.

Kreitman, Smith, and Tan (1970) in Edinburgh investigated the extent to which close friends and relatives of people who were referred to hospital following suicide attempts were themselves referred for similar behavior during a four-year period. In estimating the expected number of referrals among the "contacts" of the attempted suicide group, factors such as age, sex, and place of residence were carefully controlled. There were four times as many referrals among the "contacts," a finding compatible with, but not conclusively supporting, the hypothesis that attempted suicide occurs in social networks. Although adolescents were not specifically studied, it was noted that the finding only applied to attempters under the age of 35, especially females, and those who used drugs in their attempts.

The contagion factor is particularly likely in institutions such as schools and psychiatric hospitals. While anecdotal evidence suggests that small epidemics of minor suicidal acts sometimes occur in schools, there is more substantial evidence of such phenomena in psychiatric hospitals. Offer and Barglow (1960), for example, described in detail a series of incidents of self-mutilation carried out by a small group of 14 to 22 year old psychiatric hospital inpatients over a short period of time. The apparently competitive and imitative aspects of many of the acts were confirmed by interviews with the patients themselves. The epidemic had serious consequences for staff morale, engendering considerable feelings of anxiety and guilt. Only when a consistent approach to the problem was adopted by all the staff was the epidemic ended.

That such outbreaks should occur in psychiatric institutions is not surprising, for several reasons (Hawton, 1978). First, there is likely to be a high concentration of people with a previous history of suicidal behavior. Second, patients are usually in hospital because they are facing severe stresses, whether due to illness, social factors, or both. Suicidal acts are more likely at such times. Third, suicidal behavior usually attracts increased attention from staff. Competition for such attention may therefore lead to similar acts by other patients. Fourth, especially among adolescents, there may be a marked element of bravado that adds to the competitive element.

How such outbreaks might be contained has been discussed elsewhere (Hawton & Catalan, 1982). In brief, the key individuals involved must be identified, and, if necessary, removed from the unit. Open discussion of the behavior among the patients may help diminish its mystique. Most important, morale and communication among the staff must be maintained and a consistent management policy developed.

CONCLUSIONS

Although there are considerable problems of case definition and identification, there is clear evidence that a very dramatic increase in attempted suicide has occurred among young people in many parts of the Western world during the past two decades. This behavior is most common among girls, although attempts by children more often involve boys. In both sexes, attempted suicide occurs many times more often than completed suicide. Under the age of twelve years, attempts are rare, although by no means unknown. From the age of 12, attempted suicide becomes increasingly common. Overdoses are the usual method, and although many of these involve relatively little danger to life, others are extremely dangerous. Boys are more likely to use dangerous methods of self-injury. Outbreaks of suicide attempts may occur among adolescents in institutions, especially psychiatric hospitals. These are often sustained by competition and imitation.

6

CONTRIBUTORY FACTORS IN ATTEMPTED SUICIDE

In order to develop an understanding of why nonfatal suicidal behavior occurs in children and adolescents, three aspects require detailed consideration: first, the background characteristics and early experiences that may have increased a young person's vulnerability to resort to suicidal behavior when under stress; second, the nature of the stresses associated with an attempt, including the problems that the person is experiencing at the time of attempt and the precipitants that appear to trigger the behavior. These two aspects are the subject of this chapter. When considering background factors, problems, and precipitants it must be emphasized that inferences about causality can only be speculative; they do not by themselves provide sufficient explanation of why the behavior occurs. Thus, a third and crucial factor in explaining attempted suicide is that of motivation. This is considered in Chapter 7.

BACKGROUND CHARACTERISTICS
AND EARLY EXPERIENCES

There are four important features that are common among children and adolescents who make suicide attempts: broken homes, family psychiatric disorder, family suicidal behavior, and childhood maltreatment.

Broken Homes

A finding common to most studies of attempted suicide in children and adolescents is the large number of cases in which there is a history of a broken home (Barter et al., 1968; Bergstrand & Otto, 1962; Choquet et al., 1980; Jacobziner, 1965; Rohn et al., 1977; Stanley & Barter, 1970; Tuckman & Connon, 1962; Walker, 1980; White, 1974). This has been confirmed in studies in which comparison has been made with other young people in the general population (see Jacobs, 1971).

The author and his colleagues in Oxford studied in detail a consecutive sample of 50 adolescent self-poisoners in the age range 13 to 18, all of whom had been admitted to one general hospital following an overdose (Hawton, O'Grady et al., 1982). Half were aged between 13 and 15 years and the other half 16 to 18 years. Following the routine clinical interview by a member of the hospital psychiatric service, each adolescent was interviewed in depth by a research worker. Among many other aspects of the inquiry, the adolescents were asked about their upbringing. Of the adolescents aged 13 to 15, 36% were living with only one parent and 12% with neither parent (48% overall), compared with figures of 5% and 11.4% (16.4% overall) respectively in a sample of adolescents in the general population (Fogelman, 1976). This finding is similar to that of a Toronto study, in which 505 young attempters (aged between 6 and 20.9 years) referred to the emergency room in the Hospital for Sick Children were compared with 505 nonsuicidal control subjects, matched with the attempters for sex, age, and time of visit to the emergency department (Garfinkel et al., 1979; Garfinkel & Golombek, 1983). Compared with the control group of adolescents, the attempters had experienced three times their rate of parental separation or death, and almost twice their rate of parental divorce. Less than one-half of the attempters were now living with both parents compared with 84% of the controls. A very large proportion of the attempters' fathers were absent from the home. Most of the attempters who were separated from both their parents were living in group homes, the rate of such placement among the attempters being approximately eight times that of the controls.

An important question is to what extent are broken homes a feature of young suicide attempters compared with adolescents who develop psychiatric disorders but do not make attempts? Although absence of parents has been reported as being just as common among the latter group (Mattson, Seese, & Hawkins, 1969; Stanley & Barter, 1970), this was not found by Kosky (1983), in western Australia, when he compared 20 children under 14 years of age who had made suicide attempts with 50 psychiatrically ill nonsuicidal children, both groups having been admitted to a children's psychiatric unit. Only 40% of the parents of the suicide attempters were living together compared with 82% of the parents of the control children. Cohen-Sandler, Berman, and King (1982) reported a similar finding. There is also evidence that young suicide attempters may be distinguished from other young people with psychiatric disorders by having more often suffered *early* loss of one or both parents (Cohen-Sandler et al., 1982; Stanley & Barter, 1970).

A further factor relevant to parental absence is the nature of the situation in which the young person is placed when the parents can no longer provide adequate care. The high incidence of group home placements among the attempters studied by Garfinkel and colleagues in Toronto can be interpreted in several ways, as they themselves have pointed out (Garfinkel & Golombek, 1983): Suicidal or depressed children may be more often referred to group homes, which may tend to receive the community's most disturbed children; in that setting there may be greater exposure to suicidal children, which may facilitate the behavior (see Chapter 5); staff in such homes may have difficulty in dealing with severely disturbed children; and any children in group homes who make attempts may be more likely than attempters in the community to get referred to hospital, because of official requirements, and hence be more often detected.

Family Psychiatric Disorder

Psychiatric disorders appear to be common in the families of young suicide attempters (see, for example, Garfinkel et al., 1979; Jacobs, 1971; Walker, 1980). In Toronto, for example, a history of family psychiatric disorder was recorded for 52% of young suicide attempters compared with 16% of controls (Garfinkel et al., 1979). Alcoholism and drug abuse were the most common disorders. About 60% of the fathers with psychiatric symptoms were alcoholics, and alcoholism and drug abuse were the disorders found among a third of the mothers with psychiatric symptoms. The high incidence of alcoholism in the parents of young suicide attempters has been confirmed in other studies (e.g., Bergstrand & Otto, 1962; Cohen-Sandler et al., 1982; Rohn et al., 1977; Teicher & Jacobs, 1966). In the Toronto study, parental neurotic disorders and depression were also common, especially among the mothers. In a small series of boys aged 14 to 18 who made suicide attempts, Margolin and Teicher (1968) noted that most of their mothers were psychiatrically disturbed and themselves entertaining suicidal ideas.

Interestingly, in the Toronto study, the prevalence of psychiatric disorders among siblings did not differ much between the attempters and the controls (Garfinkel et al., 1979). A possible explanation of this finding is that genetic vulnerability to psychiatric disorder has been inherited to a greater extent by the attempters than by their siblings. The specific nature of the relationship between the attempter and his or her parents might be another.

Family Suicidal Behavior

There is substantial evidence that suicidal behavior, both fatal and nonfatal, tends to cluster within families. Teicher and Jacobs (1966) found that 44% of the 14 to 18 year old adolescents that they studied in Los Angeles had a relative or close friend who had attempted or committed suicide. Jacobs (1971) confirmed that the incidence of suicidal behavior among the relatives or friends of attempters was higher than in a control group of adolescents (among whose families no attempts were recorded). In the study by Garfinkel and colleagues (1979), previous suicidal behavior was more than seven times as frequent among members of the attempters' families compared with the families of the control subjects. Whereas completed suicide had not occurred at all in the families of the controls, eight immediate and three nonimmediate members of the families of the attempters had killed themselves; attempts were recorded for 26 family members in the attempters' group compared with only five family members in the control group.

Although the clustering of suicidal behavior within families presumably reflects the high prevalence of family psychiatric disorder noted above, suicidal acts by other family members may serve as a model for an adolescent, so that a suicidal act becomes a more readily used method of coping at a time of severe stress.

Childhood Maltreatment

Family physical abuse is relatively common among young attempters and suicidal children (Lukianowicz, 1968; Pfeffer et al., 1979; Taylor &

Stansfield, 1984). Although Pfeffer and colleagues did not find any difference between suicidal children (only a quarter of whom had made actual attempts) and age-matched psychiatrically ill controls in the extent of family abuse and violence, in a similar study in Australia Kosky (1983) reported child abuse in 60% of children who attempted suicide compared with only 4% of nonsuicidal psychiatrically ill children. Furthermore, a higher incidence of "self-destructive behavior" (such as self-biting, self-cutting, self-burning, hair pulling, head banging, suicide attempts, and suicidal threats and gestures) was found by Green (1978) in 59 abused children (49.6%) and in 29 neglected children (17.2%) compared with 30 normal controls (6.7%). The author concluded that "the abused child's sense of worthlessness, badness, and self-hatred as a consequence of parental assault, rejection, and scapegoating formed the nucleus for subsequent self-destructive behavior. The transformation of the child's self-hatred into self-destructive behavior was catalyzed by ego deficits and impaired impulse control."

A further element in this picture is the association between child abuse and parental suicidal behavior. Thus, in a study of child abuse families in the United Kingdom, Roberts and Hawton (1980) found that in 29% of the families one or both parents had made a suicide attempt. In a subsequent study of 114 mothers who made suicide attempts and who had children aged 0 to 5 years, in 6.1% of cases child abuse or neglect occurred either before the attempts or during the following year, and in a further 23.7% the children had been identified, either before the attempt or shortly after, as being at risk of abuse. No such cases were identified among a matched group of mothers from the general population. Among mothers at risk for depression, in only 4.7% was there evidence of risk of abuse, and none of actual abuse (Hawton, Roberts, & Goodwin, 1985).

Parental suicidal behavior, child abuse and neglect, and suicidal acts by children may therefore be part of a continuing cycle of internally and externally directed aggression within families.

Occasionally, parental abuse or neglect is the actual precipitant for an attempt by a young person. This was the case for 3% of the adolescents studied by Garfinkel and Golombek (1983). Now that sexual abuse of children is being increasingly recognized, it is likely that this will also emerge as an occasional precipitant of suicide attempts (Anderson, 1981).

PROBLEMS AND PRECIPITANTS
PRECEDING ATTEMPTED SUICIDE

Methodological Issues

Although often difficult, it is important to distinguish between the problems faced by young suicide attempters during the period leading up to their suicidal acts and the events that appear to precipitate the act itself. There are other obvious methodological issues involved in research into this aspect of suicidal behavior.

(1) The method by which the information is obtained is extremely important. In retrospective studies the information is usually gleaned from hospital case records. Such information is likely to be incomplete and may provide distorted findings when comparison is made with control subjects because of the very fact that a suicide attempt has occurred. For example, when suicide attempters are compared in this way with young people referred to hospital for physical illness, it should be remembered that a clinician might be more likely to look for social and psychological difficulties in the former group than in the latter. Even in prospective studies there is the question of whether information obtained from suicide attempters themselves is sufficiently reliable or whether further information should be sought from other sources such as family members, friends, and health professionals. It could be argued that the attempters themselves are the most relevant source because it is their perception of their difficulties that is most important. Ideally, however, information should be obtained from both the attempters themselves and from other sources.

(2) Another difficulty concerns the definitions of problems and precipitants. It is probably impossible to draw up entirely satisfactory criteria, and the likely differences between operational definitions must be borne in mind when comparing the findings from different studies. Furthermore, there may be important differences between problems reported by attempters themselves and those identified by clinicians and researchers. Problems related to the use of alcohol provide a good example; these are far more likely to be identified by the latter than by attempters.

(3) Finally, considerable difficulties are encountered when one tries to establish a causal link between problems or precipitants and the

actual attempts. It is essential to recognize that the association of particular types of problems with suicide attempts does not necessarily imply a causal connection. We should remind ourselves that there are likely to be many young people who have undergone similar experiences and yet *not* resorted to suicidal acts. Why this should be so is considered in the next chapter.

Nature of the Problems

Compared with nonsuicidal children and adolescents, suicide attempters are generally facing many more problems in their lives (Jacobs, 1971). The nature of their problems has been investigated in several studies. In the Oxford study of 50 adolescent self-poisoners, the research interviewer recorded each patient's problems on a standard checklist (Hawton, O'Grady et al., 1982). A problem was only recorded if it was judged to be causing difficulty for the adolescent, irrespective of whether it appeared to have a direct connection with the overdose. A disturbance in a relationship, or a mild physical complaint, for example, were only listed as problems if they seemed to be causing distress or affecting normal functioning. A second assessment of the subject's problems was made independently by the routine clinical interviewers, using the same checklist.

The nature of the problems detected by the research interviewers in this group of adolescents is summarized in Table 6.1. There was good agreement between the clinical assessors and the research interviewers concerning the adolescents' problems (Kappa = 0.578, p < 0.001). The most common problems were with parents, school or work, and with boyfriends or girlfriends. The order of problems according to their frequency in this study is in keeping with the findings of other studies both in the United Kingdom and in the United States. The different types of problems are examined more closely below, both in terms of the Oxford findings and those from elsewhere.

Relationships with Parents. The majority of child and adolescent suicide attempters who are in contact with their parents appear to face substantial difficulties in their relationships with them. Certainly, compared with adolescents in the general population, these relationships are more often disturbed. Although some people have questioned

TABLE 6.1
Current Problems Identified for 50 Adolescent Self-Poisoners

Problem Area	Percentage of Subjects for Whom Each Problem Was Applicable
Parents	76
School/work	58
Boy/girlfriend	52
Social isolation	28
Sibling(s)	22
Physical health	22
Psychiatric symptoms	20
Sexual	16
Relationship with peers	14
Alcohol	14
Physical illness of family member	14
Financial	8
Psychiatric disorder of family member	6
Legal	2
Drugs	2

SOURCE: Hawton, O'Grady, et al. (1982). Reproduced by kind permission of the editor of the *British Journal of Psychiatry*.

whether suicide attempters may differ much in this respect from psychiatrically disordered individuals who have not made a suicide attempt (Stanley & Barter, 1970), recent evidence from a London-based study suggests they do (Taylor & Stansfield, 1984). The relationship that is most often disturbed is that with the parent of the opposite sex. Among the Oxford adolescent self-poisoners, 90% of whom were girls, the main area of difficulty was typically between the girl and her father. Walker (1980) and Taylor and Stansfield (1984) have made similar observations. Most of the subjects felt totally unable to discuss any of their problems with their fathers, with whom they were also frequently in conflict. Among boys who made suicide attempts, Margolin and Teicher (1968) found that serious disturbances in the relationships between the boys and their mothers were common. Difficulties often arose because the boys found that they were expected to take over the role of the older male in the household, usually because the father was absent, and at these times they often felt nagged and unloved by their mothers. Lack of warmth among family members may be just as important a factor as actual conflict (Taylor & Stansfield, 1984).

One should not assume, of course, that conflict with, and rejection by, parents always stems from the attitudes of the parents themselves.

Child and adolescent personality difficulties may contribute to these interpersonal problems.

School or Work Difficulties. Many young suicide attempters have problems at school (Table 6.1; Garfinkel et al., 1979; Otto, 1972; Rohn et al., 1977; White, 1974). These include poor academic attainments, difficulties in relationships with teachers and/or peers, and wishing to leave school. Interestingly, Garfinkel and Golombek (1983) found that adolescents making severe (that is, dangerous) suicide attempts tended to be successful at school whereas those making less severe attempts were more likely to be failing at school. This is in keeping with the finding that children who actually kill themselves are often of superior intelligence (Shaffer, 1974).

For those who have left school, work problems are also common. In the Oxford study the unemployment rate among the 16- to 18-year-old attempters was far in excess of the unemployment rate in other young people in the Oxford area at the time of the study.

Only rarely did school or work problems appear directly to cause the attempt. More often they seemed to reflect general interpersonal difficulties and contributed to the adolescents' low self-esteem, which, in turn, probably impaired their ability to cope with other life stresses, especially those arising out of threatened relationships. In view of the association between unemployment and psychiatric disorder in teenagers (Banks & Jackson, 1982), it is possible that the currently increasing levels of unemployment among young people, especially in the United Kingdom, might lead to a further increase in attempted suicide in this age group.

Problems with Boyfriends or Girlfriends. Difficulties in the relationship with a boy- or girlfriend commonly precede suicidal acts by young people (Bergstrand & Otto, 1962; Garfinkel et al., 1979; Tuckman & Connon, 1962). The very high proportion of subjects with such problems (58%) in the Oxford study (Table 6.1) may partly have resulted from the especially large female to male ratio, for it seems that girls who make suicide attempts are more likely to have problems in their relationships with a member of the opposite sex than are boys who make attempts (Otto, 1972). Nonsupportive family relations may lead to excessively dependent relationships with members of the opposite sex; such dependence makes the individual vulnerable to overwhelming distress when the relationship is threatened or disrupted. Often the young person appears to have no one to turn to for support when in anguish about a deteriorating or disrupted relationship.

Social Isolation. This was a characteristic of only a minority of subjects in the Oxford study. In contrast with children and adolescents who kill themselves, the majority of adolescent attempters did not lack relationships, but rather their relationships were disturbed.

Siblings. Almost a quarter of the adolescents in the Oxford study had problems in their relationships with their siblings, usually because of recurrent conflicts, jealousy, or bullying.

Physical Health. In several studies of young suicide attempters, excessive numbers of subjects with poor physical health have been found (Choquet et al., 1980; Jacobs, 1971; Walker, 1980; White, 1974). This is reflected in both greater than expected numbers who have had recent general hospital admissions for physical illness and a high proportion who have current physical disorders (such as asthma or dysmenorrhea). In the Oxford study, physical illness never appeared to be directly associated with an overdose, but it often seemed to be a factor that might have increased a person's vulnerability to other stresses.

A potentially important but apparently unreplicated finding was reported by Rohn and associates (1977), who claimed that more than half of a subgroup of adolescent attempters showed evidence of minimal brain dysfunction on psychological testing. Furthermore, Struve, Klein, and Saraf (1972) found an association between EEG dysrhythmias and both suicidal thoughts and attempts among young psychiatric patients. It was suggested that such dysrhythmias might contribute to impairment of control when under stress. Clearly these findings require further investigation.

Psychiatric Disorder and Personality Factors. It is difficult to get a clear idea of the extent of psychiatric disturbance in young suicide attempters, for two reasons. First, in many studies it is unclear what criteria have been used to define psychiatric disorder. Second, there are the well-recognized problems surrounding the identification of possible depressive conditions in children and adolescents (Cantwell & Carlson,

1979; Toolan, 1962), although these difficulties are decreasing with the development of standardized measures for assessing depression in children (Carlson & Cantwell, 1982; Kovacs & Beck, 1977).

In general, relatively few young suicide attempters admitted to general hospitals appear to suffer from frank psychiatric disorders. Thus, in the Oxford study, one in five subjects had psychiatric problems, usually in the form of relatively mild depression and/or personality difficulties. In London, Taylor and Stansfield (1984) found that depression (defined according to strict criteria) was more common among adolescent self-poisoners (26%) than among nonsuicidal adolescents referred to an adolescent psychiatry service (2%). Studies in which children and adolescents referred to psychiatric units following suicide attempts have been investigated have, not surprisingly, shown far higher rates of psychiatric disorders and symptoms, depression and affective symptoms being the most common (Clarkin, Friedman, Hurt, Corn, & Aronoff, 1984). Psychiatric disorders appear to be more common among boys than girls. In the large series of young attempters studied in Sweden, for example, Otto (1972) found that 35.7% of the boys had psychiatric disorders, compared with 14.1% of the girls. The most common conditions were neuroses and character disorders, with a few subjects suffering from schizophrenia.

Because of the close link between affective disorder and adult suicidal behavior (Barraclough, Bunch, Nelson, & Sainsbury, 1974; Guze & Robins, 1970), the relationship between depression and suicidal behavior in young people warrants closer examination. As Carlson and Cantwell (1982) have noted, the relationship is complex. When these authors used a standardized measure of depression, the Children's Depression Inventory, and measures of suicidal ideation and behavior, to study a series of children and adolescents referred to a psychiatric unit, they found that suicidal ideation increased around puberty (a finding that is examined more closely in the next chapter) and correlated with severity of depression. However, the link between depression and suicidal behavior is not straightforward. When a third parameter, hopelessness, is examined, it appears that this is the important factor that is associated with both suicidal ideation and suicidal behavior, not depression per se (Kazdin, French, Unis, Esveldt-Dawson, & Sherick, 1983). This is consistent with earlier findings from studies of adult suicide attempters (Beck, Kovacs, & Weissman, 1975; Wetzel, 1976).

However, it is also important to recognize that suicidal behavior often occurs in young people in the absence of depression. Indeed, in the study by Carlson and Cantwell (1982), only slightly more of the depressed children and adolescents had made attempts compared with the nondepressed individuals. The majority of adolescent suicide attempts appear to be related to "adjustment reactions" or "adolescent crises" (see, for example, Mattsson et al., 1969; White, 1974). Certainly this appeared to be the case in the adolescents in the Oxford study (Hawton, O'Grady, et al., 1982).

High rates of serious alcohol abuse have been reported in some studies of adolescent suicide attempters (see Headlam, Goldsmith, Hanenson, & Rauh, 1979). This was not found in the Oxford study, although a small proportion appeared to have problems with the use of alcohol (Table 6.1).

Personality factors that might characterize groups of young suicide attempters have not been studied extensively. On the basis of the results of arithmetical and problem-solving tests, Levenson and Neuringer (1971) reported that suicidal adolescents showed diminished problem-solving capacity compared with matched control subjects. White (1974) suggested that adolescent suicide attempters showed greater neuroticism traits than the normal population.

Sexual Problems. Only occasionally do sexual problems appear to be directly linked with attempted suicide. It seems unlikely that the 16% of adolescents in the Oxford study who were thought to have sexual problems (Table 6.1) would have represented a very different proportion from that which might be found among adolescents in general.

It has occasionally been suggested that teenage pregnancy is a common reason for suicide attempts by girls (Mattsson et al., 1969). More reports, however, suggest that it is not (Otto, 1972; White, 1974). Fear of pregnancy was certainly not a common factor among the girls in the Oxford study—only two (4%) reported being concerned that they might be pregnant, and both had a negative pregnancy test while in hospital. It is likely that at any one time a similar proportion of teenage girls in the general population would also have fears concerning possible pregnancy. There is, however, evidence that a history of *previous* pregnancy is more common among girls who make suicide attempts than among girls in the general population (Bernstein, 1972; Jacobs, 1971).

None of the adolescents in the Oxford series expressed anxieties concerning homosexuality. Presumably such fears occasionally lead to suicide attempts, especially among boys, although increasingly permissive attitudes toward homosexuality may have made this less likely.

Physical Illness in Family Members. Medical problems appear to be particularly common in the families of young suicide attempters. In the Oxford study, illness in one or the other parent appeared to cause problems for several adolescents (Table 6.1). Garfinkel and Golombek (1983) found that, when compared with control adolescents, an excessive proportion of the adolescent attempters had family members with physical problems. The difference was most marked among the fathers, who tended in particular to suffer from chronic and debilitating illness (such as cardiovascular disease, diabetes, organic brain syndromes, and orthopedic disorders). However, no difference was found between the prevalence of physical disorders among the siblings of the attempters and those of the controls.

Parental physical illness may affect adolescents in two ways. First, the adolescent may be concerned about the parent's ill-health, especially when the condition is life-threatening. Second, parents with chronic handicaps may not pay sufficient attention to the emotional needs of their children, being more concerned with their own plight, and in particular may be unable to provide support when the adolescent is under stress. Furthermore, the adolescent may be unwilling to seek the help of such a parent at a time of crisis for fear of imposing yet another burden.

Psychiatric Disorder in Family Members. The high incidence of psychiatric disorders in the parents of young suicide attempters has already been discussed. The problems posed by a parent with a chronic neurotic or psychotic disorder, or one with a drinking problem, may contribute to suicide attempts in some cases (Table 6.1). Very occasionally, a young person will make an attempt as a desperate response to having to cope with a schizophrenic parent.

Drug Problems. It was surprising that only one out of the 50 adolescent self-poisoners in the Oxford study had a problem related to the use of drugs. Garfinkel and Golombek (1983) reported "street drug use" in over a third of their adolescent attempters in Toronto compared with just over 5% of control subjects. They did not comment on how often such drug use was problematical. High rates of drug abuse were also found in another North American study, with especially high rates among boys (Headlam et al., 1979). Differences in findings concerning drug abuse are likely to represent general variations in drug use between different areas and countries. It often appears that drug abuse itself is a suicidal equivalent, especially when the drugs involved are dangerous and these dangers are known to the adolescent. Distinguishing deliberate self-poisoning from an accidental overdose of drugs is often not easy, and may be somewhat arbitrary, especially when the intent in both cases may be temporary oblivion and escape from current stress.

Accumulation of Stress

Earlier work on adult suicide attempters in the United States demonstrated that they experienced more stressful life events during the six months preceding their attempts than did both depressed psychiatric inpatients in the six months prior to their admission to hospital and general population controls over a similar time period (Paykel, Prusoff, & Myers, 1975). In a comparison of child and adolescent suicide attempers, depressed nonsuicidal individuals, and nondepressed psychiatric controls, all of whom were admitted to a psychiatric inpatient unit, Cohen-Sandler and associates (1982) clearly demonstrated a similar finding for the 12-month period preceding hospital admission. The suicide attempters had experienced twice as much stress (measured on a scale of social readjustment or adaptation) as had the young people in the other two groups. Furthermore, earlier in their lives the suicide attempters had experienced increasing and significantly greater amounts of stress as they had matured through various developmental stages. Especially common stresses were chaotic and disruptive family events that resulted in losses and separations from important people, particularly parents and other relatives.

Classification of Young Suicide Attempters

It will be obvious to the reader that children and adolescents who make suicide attempts are an extremely heterogeneous group of individuals. From the clinical, as well as the theoretical point of view, it is therefore important to try to categorize them into subgroups according to their background characteristics, problems, and, if possible, outcome. A simple method was devised for classifying the adolescent self-poisoners in the Oxford study (Hawton, Osborn, O'Grady, & Cole, 1982). It consists of three categories, which are defined by the duration of the patient's problems and the presence or absence of behavioral disturbances:

Group 1: Acute. The problems identified at the time of the overdose have persisted for less than one month; absence of behavioral disturbance.

Group 2: Chronic. The problems identified at the time of the overdose have persisted for one month or more; absence of behavioral disturbance.

Group 3: Chronic with Behavioral Disturbance. The problems identified at the time of the overdose have persisted for one month or more; there has been recent behavioral disturbance (such as stealing, repeated truancy, drug taking, heavy drinking, fighting, or being in trouble with the police).

When the three groups were compared on various factors concerning the adolescents' backgrounds, family relationships, and current problems, some marked differences emerged. These are summarized in Table 6.2. Thus there was an increase in the extent of family pathology from subjects in Group 1 (Acute) through those in Group 2 (Chronic) to those in Group 3 (Chronic with behavior disturbance). The number of problems identified per adolescent increased from Group 1 to Group 3. The problems of the adolescents in Group 1 were almost entirely confined to difficulties in current relationships, whereas the problems of those in the other two groups were much more diverse. The adolescents with medical or psychiatric pathology were largely in Groups 2 and 3, and especially in the latter.

This very simple classification scheme requires further investigation. The only other classification of this kind appears to be that of Choquet and colleagues (1980) in France. On the basis of cluster analysis, they distinguished four subgroups. Direct comparison between their scheme and that developed in the Oxford study is difficult because they included

TABLE 6.2

Characteristics of Adolescent Self-Poisoners Categorized
According to a Simple Classification Scheme

	Classification		
	Group 1 "Acute"	Group 2 "Chronic"	Group 3 "Chronic with Behavior Disturbance"
Broken homes		+	+++
Family history of psychiatric disorder			+++
Poor relationship with parents:			
Mother		+	+++
Father	+	++	+++
Previous psychiatric disorder or treatment		+	+++
Previous overdose/self-injury			++
Number of problems	+	++	+++
Psychiatric symptoms		+	+++

NOTE: The + signs indicate the extent to which characteristic is displayed by members of each group.

some older subjects. Thus their first group includes males usually aged 19 and over who had made serious attempts and came from a background of severe psychopathology. Their second group (which seemed to differ little from their first group) was very like Group 3 (Chronic with behavior disturbance) in the Oxford study, being characterized by "unfavorable sociofamilial factors" and more psychiatric problems. Their third group included many adolescents who had only mild to moderately disturbed upbringings and made their attempts in response to emotional and health problems. This group, while appearing to overlap somewhat with Group 2 (Chronic) in the Oxford study, did not closely resemble any of the three groups in that study. On the other hand, adolescents in the fourth group in the French study seemed to be very similar to those in Group 1 (Acute) in the Oxford study, being mostly girls from relatively normal backgrounds.

While helping to separate adolescent attempters into meaningful categories, especially with regard to outcome and repetition of attempts, classifying adolescents in this way also raises some important questions. The most obvious is why should adolescents in Group 1 (Acute) take overdoses at all, because they do not appear to differ from many adolescents in the general population. This question is considered further in the next chapter.

Precipitants

Most studies are in agreement as to the common precipitants of attempts by young people, namely conflicts with family members, disruption in a relationship with a boyfriend or girlfriend, conflicts with a member of the individual's peer group, and school difficulties (Garfinkel & Golombek, 1983; Hawton, O'Grady, et al., 1982; Jacobziner, 1965; Mattsson et al., 1969; White, 1974).

Occasionally the apparent precipitant of a suicide attempt is an overwhelming stress, such as death of a family member. However, often the precipitant appears to be relatively trivial or insufficient to explain why the attempt occurred. This is because the precipitant for the act may represent a "final straw," which, on top of more severe long-standing problems, finally tips the balance and pushes the individual beyond his or her threshold between constraints against and forces acting toward suicidal behavior.

Not all attempts follow a clear precipitant. In the Oxford study, in which a precipitant was defined as a tangible event during the 48 hours preceding the act that appeared to bear a direct link with the attempt, no such precipitant could be identified in a third of cases (Hawton, O'Grady, et al., 1982b). Absence of an obvious precipitant is more likely when the attempt occurs in the setting of a depressive illness, the attempt then often being motivated by ideas of worthlessness and hopelessness rather than representing a direct response to an external event.

CONCLUSIONS

Several aspects of the family background and early life of young suicide attempters may contribute to their eventual suicidal behavior. These include broken homes, family psychiatric disorder and suicidal acts, and childhood maltreatment. A variety of problems and precipitants may be associated with the attempts, with difficulties with parents, boyfriends or girlfriends, and school or work being especially common. A means of classifying adolescent suicide attempters has been described. It appears possible to distinguish subgroups of individuals that differ markedly in their backgrounds and problems. One hopes this approach will undergo further development because it could have important clinical as well as theoretical implications. As will be discussed in later chapters, these include planning of management strategies and prediction of outcome.

7

MOTIVATIONAL ASPECTS OF SUICIDAL BEHAVIOR

Unraveling the motivational aspects of suicidal behavior in young people, or in adults for that matter, is extremely complicated. One very important factor, especially in younger adolescents and children, concerns the concept of death, including the way in which it develops, the age at which this concept matures, and possible differences in attitudes toward death among suicidal and nonsuicidal individuals. This is therefore the first topic to be considered in this chapter.

As noted in the previous chapter, our understanding of suicidal behavior will be far from complete if attention is only paid to the problems and precipitants that have led up to it. The motivational aspects of the behavior must also be explored. Essentially, "motivation" refers to the intention behind the behavior, but usually this is not directly accessible, and is therefore difficult to study. Often a person's intention appears to be unconscious, or, if conscious, it may be too difficult for the person to admit to the true intention because of fear of condemnation by family members, friends, and health professionals. It is hardly surprising therefore that so little research has been directed toward elucidating motivation for attempted suicide. This is unfortunate because such understanding is likely to be crucial if effective methods of prevention are to be devised. The rest of this chapter is therefore devoted to this important area of study. In particular, the following topics will be explored: how suicide attempts are explained, both by attempters themselves and by other people; the circumstances in which the behavior occurs; and the premeditation involved. Finally, drawing on the findings that have been discussed, a theoretical model will be put forward to explain suicidal behavior by children and adolescents.

CONCEPT OF DEATH

Considerable attention has been devoted to the question of how and when children develop a concept of death, especially in terms of death being both an irreversible and universal phenomenon. Clearly this is of considerable relevance when trying to understand suicidal behavior in children and adolescents. It appears that full awareness of the finality of death does not usually develop until around the age of 12 years (Koocher, 1974; Piaget, 1960). Very young children appear to regard death as a reversible process in which bodily functions, like seeing and hearing, persist. Some notion of irreversibility begins to develop between the ages of five and nine years, and it is only after the age of nine that this concept matures. There seems to be some correlation between the acquisition of the notion of death as a universal phenomenon (that it will happen to everyone) and general cognitive development (White, Elsom, & Prawat, 1978).

The immaturity of the concept of death in younger children could be a major factor in explaining why suicidal behavior is relatively rare under the age 12 years. Shaffer and Fisher (1981) have also suggested other factors that may be relevant to the rarity of suicidal behavior until early adolescence, including a low incidence of depression in children, their close integration within the family, and the necessity for a significant degree of cognitive maturity to have developed before a child can develop feelings such as despair and hopelessness. Furthermore, the capacity to plan ahead is important in suicidal behavior, and this also does not develop until later childhood.

Attitudes Toward Death Among Suicidal Individuals

This brings us to the question of whether there are any differences in attitudes to death between suicidal and normal children. As might be expected, children who have engaged in or threatened suicidal acts are more preoccupied with thoughts about death than are nonsuicidal children (Pfeffer et al., 1979; Pfeffer, Conte, Plutchik, & Jerrett, 1980). Interestingly, Pfeffer and her colleagues found that death was viewed as both a temporary and a pleasant phenomenon more commonly by suicidal children (few of whom had made actual attempts) admitted to an inpatient psychiatry unit than among nonsuicidal children admitted to the unit, but no differences were found in these attitudes between suicidal and nonsuicidal children who were psychiatric outpatients. This discrepancy may have reflected differences in the extent of psychopathology between the inpatient and outpatient groups.

An important contribution to the understanding of attitudes to death in suicidal children has been provided by Orbach, Carlson, Feshbach, Glaubman, and Gross (1983), who distiguished between attraction and repulsion by both life and death. They used a technique involving children's responses to questions about stories to investigate these four parameters (attraction to life, repulsion by life, attraction to death, repulsion by death). The stories concerned situations involving a dilemma regarding life or death that were judged by the authors to tap each of these four attitudes. The heroes of the stories were animals, and death and dying were represented through the hero's transformation into an inanimate object and vice versa. Suicidal children, in contrast to normal children, shared a high degree of repulsion by life and attraction to death and a relatively low degree of attraction to life and repulsion by death. At the same time there was considerable conflict in attitudes among the suicidal children, especially in their attitudes to life, in that they were both attracted to life as well as repulsed by it.

Further work is clearly required to elucidate the concept of death among children and adolescents who engage in suicidal acts or entertain suicidal ideas. This may have important implications for the treatment of such young people, especially in terms of developing possible cognitive approaches to management.

HOW SUICIDE ATTEMPTS ARE EXPLAINED BY ADOLESCENTS AND OTHER PEOPLE

Various methods can be used when seeking explanations for suicidal acts by adolescents. One approach is to ask them directly to account for their suicide attempts. A limitation of this approach is that a patient's explanation may change shortly after the attempt (Bergstrand & Otto, 1962; Leese, 1969; White, 1974). Another difficulty is that an individual may be unable to explain the behavior spontaneously; this was the case in 54% of the adolescent self-poisoners studied by White (1974). One method of overcoming this problem, which is described below, is to ask the patient to choose reasons from a list of possibilities. A further approach that will be discussed is the use of the repertory grid technique (Parker, 1981).

Feelings Preceding Attempts

In the study of adolescent self-poisoners in Oxford (Hawton, Cole, et al., 1982), the states of mind preceding the overdoses were examined by asking the adolescents to select from a series of five printed cards those which best described how they had been feeling at the time of the attempt (Table 7.1). They could choose more than one if necessary. Just over half the adolescents indicated that they had been angry with someone or feeling lonely or unwanted. These feelings are congruent with the problems that were noted in the previous chapter to commonly precede self-poisoning; for example, poor communication with parents and disruption in the relationship with a boy or girlfriend. They are also compatible, as discussed below, with the explanations that the adolescents most commonly gave for their overdoses. Compared with the younger adolescents (13 to 15 years), significantly more of the older subjects (16 to 18 years) indicated that they had been feeling worried about the future. This may have been the result of the older adolescents being more aware of the way in which their lives were developing. It may also have reflected greater feelings of hopelessness in the older adolescents, although this association was not specifically examined in this study.

As mentioned in the previous chapter, it is now recognized that a sense of hopelessness, rather than general depression, is a major factor in determining suicidal behavior. Kazdin and colleagues (1983) have demonstrated the same phenomenon in a sample of children aged 8 to 13 years, which included some who had made attempts and others who had only entertained suicidal ideas. Thus, suicidal intent was more consistently correlated with hopelessness than with depression. Furthermore, Topol and Reznikoff (1982) have demonstrated a greater degree of hopelessness in hospitalized adolescents who had made suicide attempts than in similar adolescents who had not made attempts.

TABLE 7.1
Feelings That 50 Adolescent Self-Poisoners Reported
Having at the Time of Their Overdoses

| | Age Group | | |
	Under 16 (N = 25)	16-18 (N = 25)	Both (N = 50)
Feelings			
Angry with someone	15 (60%)	12 (48%)	27 (54%)
Lonely or unwanted	13 (52%)	14 (56%)	27 (54%)
Worried about the future	6 (24%)	14 (56%)*	20 (40%)
Failed in life	4 (16%)	10 (40%)	14 (28%)
Sorry or ashamed of something	2 (8%)	5 (20%)	7 (14%)

*x^2 = 4.08, df = 1, p < 0.05.
SOURCE: Hawton, Cole, et al. (1982). Reproduced by kind permission of the editor of the *British Journal of Psychiatry*.

Reasons Given to Explain Attempted Suicide

There has been little in the way of systematic investigation of the explanations for this behavior in young people. Many authors have conjectured about likely reasons, but have not subjected their theories to empirical testing. Others have asked the adolescents to give spontaneous explanations for their attempts, which, as noted earlier, they may find difficult. Thus, White (1974) found that 54% of the 50 adolescent self-poisoners in his study where unable or unwilling to say what they hoped to achieve by taking the overdose, or provided some vague explanation such as "it just came over me," or "I was fed up." For the 23 patients who where able to provide some more definite explanation, White classified their responses as follows: "death" (11 subjects), "influence others" (6), "escape" (3), "sleep" (2), and "procure abortion" (1).

In the Oxford study of 50 adolescent self-poisoners, the reasons given both by the adolescents themselves and by the clinical staff involved in their care were examined (Hawton, Cole, et al., 1982). This investigation will be described in some detail because it sheds considerable light on this important aspect of attempted suicide in young people.

The adolescents were first asked about their suicidal intent at the time of the overdose, by requesting each to select one from a series of three cards to indicate whether, at the time of the act, the subject had (a) wanted to die; (b) didn't want to die; or (c) didn't mind whether lived or died. The member of the clinical service who had carried out the routine

TABLE 7.2
Suicidal Intent Among 50 Adolescent Self-Poisoners:
Self-Report Versus Clinicians' Assessment

	Wanted to Die	Did Not Mind Whether Lived or Died	Did Not Want to Die
Selected by the adolescents (N = 50)	17 (54%)	21 (42%)	12 (24%)
Selected by the clinicians	7 (14%)	9 (18%)	34 (68%)
Number of times clinicians agreed with the adolescents (percentage of adolescents' choice)	5 (29%)	6 (29%)	12 (100%)

SOURCE: Hawton, Cole, et al. (1982). Reproduced by kind permission of the editor of the *British Journal of Psychiatry*.
NOTE: Clinicians' versus adolescents' choices χ^2 = 19.49, df = 2, p < 0.001.

clinical assessment of each case was also asked to indicate his or her impression of the subject's suicidal intent in the same way (Table 7.2). A highly significant difference was found between the adolescents' choices and those of the clinical assessors. Many more of the adolescents indicated that they had wanted to die (34%) than were judged by the clinicians to have felt this way (14%). Similarly, more of the adolescents indicated that they had been ambivalent or did not mind whether they lived or died (42%) than were so judged by the clinical staff (18%). The clinical assessors considered that the majority of the adolescents had *not* wanted to die (68% compared with only 24% of the adolescents). Complete agreement between the adolescents and the clinicians was found in all cases in which the patients indicated no suicidal intent at all, but the clinicians only agreed with five (29%) of the adolescents who said they had wanted to die. The interesting discrepancy between the choices of the adolescents and those of the clinical staff is discussed below.

In order to investigate further explanations for the behavior (other than the "wish to die"), each adolescent was asked to select from a series of eight printed cards those which best described his or her reasons for taking the overdose. The reasons are listed in Table 7.3. As many reasons could be chosen as thought necessary to explain the act. Again the clinical assessor in each case also selected reasons he or she thought best explained the behavior by choosing from the same list of eight that was offered to the adolescents.

TABLE 7.3

Reasons (other than suicidal intent) Selected by
50 Adolescents and Their Clinical Assessors to
Explain the Adolescents' Overdoses

Reasons	Selected by the Adolescents (N = 50)	Selected by the Clinical Assessors (N = 50)	Comparison of the Numbers of Clinical Assessors' and Adolescents' Choices
(a) Get relief from a terrible state of mind	21 (42%)	20 (40%)	n.s.
(b) Escape for a while from an impossible situation	21 (42%)	18 (36%)	n.s.
(c) Make people understand how desperate you were feeling	21 (42%)	30 (60%)	n.s
(d) Make people sorry for the way they have treated you, frighten or get back at someone	16 (32%)	28 (56%)	$x^2 = 8.103$, $p < 0.01$
(e) Try to influence some particular person to get them to change their mind	13 (26%)	28 (56%)	$x^2 = 4.911$, $p < 0.05$
(f) Show how much you loved someone	13 (26%)	8 (16%)	n.s.
(g) Find out whether someone really loved you or not	12 (24%)	9 (18%)	n.s.
(h) Seek help from someone	9 (18%)	19 (38%)	$x^2 = 4.018$, $p < 0.05$

SOURCE: Hawton, Cole, et al. (1982). Reproduced by kind permission of the editor of the *British Journal of Psychiatry.*

The frequencies with which the adolescents and the clinical assessors chose these other reasons to explain the overdoses are shown in Table 7.3. The reasons most often chosen by the patients (*a, b,* and *c*) suggested that the adolescents were in a distressed state and/or a very stressful situation prior to the overdose. The clinical assessors also frequently selected the first two reasons (*a* and *b*), but chose the third reason (*c*) somewhat more frequently than the adolescents.

One striking difference between the adolescents' choices and those of the clinicians was that the latter far more frequently selected the punitive and manipulative reasons (*d* and *e*) than did the adolescents. This discrepancy was also found, though to an even more marked extent, in a similar study of adult self-poisoning patients (Bancroft et al., 1979). The difference between the reasons chosen by the adolescents and those selected by the clinicians may have arisen because some adolescents recognized that admitting to punitive or manipulative reasons was likely to evoke unfavorable attitudes from hospital staff (Hawton et al., 1981; Ramon, Bancroft, & Skrimshire, 1975). A more likely explanation, however, is that many overdoses with punitive or manipulative explanations are an unconscious expression of externally directed hostility that is unrecognized by the patient. The large number of cases in which suicidal intention is claimed by the adolescent but not apparent to the clinician suggests that "wanting to die" often provides the only reason for taking an overdose that seems credible or legitimate to the patient. Thus, adolescent self-poisoners may feel so distressed at the time of taking the overdose that they feel *as if* they want to die, but death is not the (unconsciously) intended outcome of the act. "Wanting to die" may be the individual's way of legitimizing the suicide attempt in his or her own mind. However, it is also essential to realize that in some cases suicidal intention will be serious and will be the main reason for the act (that is, the attempt may be a failed suicide).

Another important difference between adolescent and clinician in this study was that the clinical assessors more often judged the overdose to be a means of obtaining help (reason *h*) than did the adolescents. The "cry for help" hypothesis for many suicide attempts was first put forward by Stengel and Cook (1958). However, this may be a misleading explanation because it implies that the suicide attempter may be trying to seek professional help. A more apposite explanation was provided by White (1974) who, when commenting on Stengel and Cook's idea, said of adolescent overdoses: "Today, some self-poisoning episodes may still have an appeal function, but the appeal is more often interpersonal than directed to any outside helping agency. The patient wishes to modify the outlook of those close to her." This may explain why many adolescent self-poisoners initially reject any offer of professional help. Unfortunately, this rejection is often misunderstood by clinicians who may consequently be annoyed by an individual's initial failure to accept help, thus further alienating the person and making engagement in constructive treatment highly unlikely. A sucessful treatment alliance would be more easily established if the clinician first acknowledged that the attempt was not made in order to get professional help, and then went on to explore with the individual how he or she might be assisted in dealing with the difficulties that led to the overdose.

A final point is that the motivation for attempted suicide is usually complex. This is evidenced by the finding in the Oxford study that in most cases both the adolescents and the clinicians attributed the overdose to more than one reason, often several.

A further study that is of relevance to this aspect of self-poisoning is Parker's (1981), which employed the repertory grid technique to compare how overdoses in general were perceived by young people who took overdoses with low suicidal intent and those who took overdoses with high suicidal intent. Whereas the high intent group perceived "an overdose" and "suicide" in quite similar terms, the low intent group perceived an overdose as similar to "being alone and crying" and "getting drunk," and construed it almost exclusively as an escape from tension. In fact the low intent group perceived an overdose as second only to getting drunk as an easy course of action. Other possible actions, such as seeking professional help, or talking to a key person, were perceived as very much less easy. Parker concluded that for many young self-poisoners, especially those with low suicidal intent, an overdose serves a "respite" function, allowing the person to escape, albeit temporarily, from distressing circumstances. This is in keeping with two of the three reasons chosen most frequently by the adolescents in the Oxford study, namely to "get relief from a terrible state of mind," and "to escape for a while from an impossible situation."

CIRCUMSTANCES OF THE ACT

Important clues about the intention involved in an overdose or self-injury are to be found in the circumstances in which the act occurs. These include any practical planning for the act, precautions that are taken to avoid or to ensure discovery, leaving a suicide note, the timing of the act, whether other people are in the vicinity when the act occurs, and whether potential helpers are notified after the act. In the Oxford study of adolescent self-poisoners (Hawton, Cole, et al., 1982), the circumstances surrounding the overdoses rarely suggested that they were seriously intended to result in death. As can be seen from Table 7.4, it was unusual to find evidence that the overdoses had been planned, and they usually occurred in circumstances that ensured that the adolescents would be discovered and receive medical attention. In most cases someone was in the vicinity, often in a nearby room.

However, although the majority of overdoses may follow this pattern, this should not obscure the fact that in a few cases attempts are

TABLE 7.4
Circumstances of 50 Adolescents' Overdoses

		(N = 50)
(1)	Evidence of any planning for the overdose	10 (20%)
(2)	Left a suicide note	6 (12%)
(3)	Precautions taken to prevent discovery and intervention by other people	3 (6%)
(4)	Overdose timed so that intervention was very likely	39 (78%)
(5)	Someone present or nearby (for instance, in the next room)	43 (86%)
(6)	Notified potential helper after the overdose	43 (86%)

SOURCE: Hawton, Cole, et al. (1982). Reproduced by kind permission of the editor of the *British Journal of Psychiatry*.

made in circumstances in which discovery is unlikely. For these adolescents the suicidal intent is likely to be high. Furthermore, in appraising the intention involved in suicidal acts in which the method used was highly dangerous and the adolescent was aware of the dangers involved, greater attention should be paid to the nature of the act than to the circumstances in which it occurred.

Premeditation

Several authors have commented on the highly impulsive nature of many overdoses and self-injuries by young people (Jacobziner, 1965; Walker, 1980; White, 1974). In the Oxford study (Hawton, Cole, et al., 1982), over half the adolescent self-poisoners reported thinking seriously about the act for less than a quarter of an hour, and 16% for a period between 15 minutes and an hour. Only 8% had contemplated taking the overdose for more than 24 hours. There was little difference in the reported duration of premeditation between the younger and older adolescents. In another British study, three-quarters of a group of adolescent self-poisoners had contemplated taking their overdoses for less than two hours (Taylor & Stansfield, 1984). Such figures do not mean that suicidal behavior had never been considered in the past. Indeed, as will be suggested later, it is likely that some sort of cognitive rehearsal of the behavior has often occurred long beforehand. Furthermore, the amount of premeditation recorded in these studies did not include time spent with vague suicidal thoughts, such as "I hope I do not wake up in the morning." In general, however, the longer a *particular* act has been contemplated the more serious the suicidal intent is likely to be.

A THEORETICAL MODEL OF ATTEMPTED SUICIDE
IN CHILDREN AND ADOLESCENTS

An important factor in understanding suicidal behavior in children and adolescents, as discussed at the beginning of this chapter, is the way in which the concept of death is developed. It was noted that awareness that death is a final event does not begin to develop substantially until between the ages of 9 and 11 years, and full awareness of the concept of death does not usually occur until early adolescence. In the ideation of suicidal children, death may be viewed as being a temporary and pleasant state offering relief from pain (Pfeffer et al., 1979), and this may facilitate suicidal behavior when the child is under severe stress. For most children, their immature awareness of death is probably protective and may explain in part way suicidal behavior is relatively rare until the age of 12 years. Integration within the family and the rarity of childhood depression (Kashani et al., 1983) may be other factors.

It has been noted that most suicide attempts by adolescents appear to be impulsive. However, a great deal of vague ideation may have occurred at other times of stress, possibly several years beforehand, and this may serve as a form of "cognitive rehearsal" that allows the concept of a suicidal act to be activated rapidly at a time of severe stress. Such ideation is typified in a common childhood fantasy in response to conflict with parents: "You will be sorry when I am dead. . . . You will see how badly you treated me." Interestingly, this thought encapsulates the clinician's explanations for many of the adolescents' overdoses in the Oxford study, as was discussed earlier. Evidence concerning the prevalence of suicidal ideation in young adolescents comes from a survey by Bagley (1975), who found that among 112 boys and 128 girls in a comprehensive school in southern England, 4.5% of the boys and 9.4% of the girls admitted to having experienced *relatively serious suicidal ideation* at some time.

Suicidal ideation is related to the individual's prevailing mood and circumstances, which are, of course, closely interrelated. For example, Friedrich, Reams, and Jacobs (1982) found that among junior high school adolescents, aged 13 to 16 years, scores on the Beck Depression Inventory, a well-established measure of depression (Beck, Ward, & Mendelson, 1961), were related to family cohesion and evidence of life stress. The adolescents' scores on the suicidal ideation item within the Depression Inventory were also related to measures of the family environment, including degree of cohesion. These findings are in keeping with the disturbed family backgrounds and current family environments found in adolescent suicide attempters, as were discussed in the previous chapter.

There remains, however, the tantalizing question of what factors distinguish the young person who crosses the threshold between entertaining suicidal thoughts and actually engaging in suicidal behavior from other young people who have entertained similar ideas but never put them into practice. The following are possible contributory factors:

(1) It has been suggested that disturbed upbringing may impair personality formation resulting characteristically in poor impulse control, lability of mood, and a defective sense of reality (Pfeffer et al., 1979).

(2) Suicidal behavior in other persons, especially other family members and friends, may provide a model of coping for the adolescent to copy. Occasionally, competition between individual family members or between friends may even provoke suicidal acts.

(3) Some adolescents may readily become hopeless when faced with stress, and this, as was noted earlier, appears to be an important link between depressive feelings and both suicidal ideation and suicidal behavior in adults (Beck, Beck, & Kovacs, 1975) and adolescents (Kazdin et al., 1983). There may be increased vulnerability to developing feelings of hopelessness among adolescents who have experienced markedly negative events (parental separation, for example) earlier in life.

(4) A crucial point beyond which suicidal behavior becomes more likely may be when life appears particularly unattractive and death seems attractive. Considerable ambivalence about living is, however, common, and may partly explain the low suicidal intent of many attempts.

(5) Alcohol consumption may lead to disinhibition and contribute both to impulsive suicidal acts and to the enactment of longer term suicidal thoughts.

(6) In recent years, the use of mood-altering medication to deal with dysphoric feelings, even when these are the result of social and interpersonal difficulties, has become increasingly common. This may facilitate the taking of an excess of such medication when faced by apparently overwhelming stress.

(7) Because prescribed or nonprescribed medication is readily available in most homes, the adolescent may not have to look beyond the bathroom cupboard for the means of an overdose; thus there need be little delay between the decision to take an overdose and actually doing so. Means of

self-injury are also often readily available, although there are marked differences both between countries and within countries in the availability of certain methods (such as firearms).

CONCLUSIONS

Extremely complex issues are encountered when one tries to examine the motivational aspects of suicidal behavior. The development in children and adolescents of the ill-understood concept of death appears to be an important factor. This concept is not usually well developed until around the age of 12 and this may partly explain why suicidal behavior is much rarer in children than in adolescents. Nevertheless, unrealistic attitudes toward death in children may also explain some childhood suicidal behavior. Further work, aimed at clarifying how attitudes to death differ between distressed adolescents who make attempts and similar adolescents who do not, is now required.

The main feelings that appear to precede attempts by adolescents are anger, feeling lonely or unwanted, and worries about the future. A sense of hopelessness is a major factor distinguishing depressed adolescents who make attempts from similar adolescents who do not.

Marked differences are found in the ways in which attempts are explained by adolescents themselves and how they are explained by other people, both in terms of suicidal intent and other explanations. Apart from suicidal intent, adolescents commonly explain the behavior as a means of alleviating or escaping from intolerable stress and of demonstrating their distress to other people. Clinicians, while agreeing that escaping from stressful situations and demonstrating distress to others are common reasons, are especially likely to interpret suicidal attempts as punitive or manipulative, and as a means of getting help. These differences in explanations for the behavior may have important implications for management, as will be discussed later.

The circumstances of many attempts by adolescents do not suggest high suicidal intent, although caution must be exercised when making such judgments in individual cases, especially when the method used in the attempt is in itself dangerous. Often there has been little premeditation preceding the attempt, a fact that, as we will see later, may pose problems when one considers means of prevention.

This chapter has ended with an incomplete explanation of the factors that may contribute to suicidal acts by young people. This is an important area for further research, although complex methodological issues must be overcome if further progress and understanding are to ensue.

8

MANAGEMENT OF CHILDREN AND ADOLESCENTS FOLLOWING SUICIDE ATTEMPTS

This chapter concerns the provision of help for young people who have been referred to hospitals, either general or psychiatric, following suicide attempts. The principles discussed, however, are just as relevant to family doctors or professionals in nonhospital settings. Before any therapeutic plan can be established, a thorough assessment must be carried out. The chapter therefore begins with a description of a well-proven assessment procedure, including general principles as well as specific guidelines. The second half of the chapter is devoted to treatment approaches. Because a detailed description of all aspects of treatment would itself necessitate more than a complete book, only the main elements of therapy will be discussed.

ASSESSMENT

Before examining details of the assessment of young people who have made suicide attempts, some important general principles require emphasis.

General Aspects of the Assessment

The management of young persons who have taken overdoses or deliberately injured themselves is often grossly inadequate. The initial assessment after hospital referral may be a rushed and superficial affair, undertaken by busy and sometimes unsympathetic emergency room staff (Jacobs, 1971; Ramon et al., 1975), their primary aim, understandably, being to deal with the physical complications of the suicide attempt. However, the individual's psychosocial problems may then be neglected and the patient may be discharged without adequate plans for further care.

Ideally, when a young suicide attempter is referred to a general hospital, he or she should be admitted to a hospital bed to allow time for a full assessment. Where shortage of hospital beds or the triviality of the attempt make admission inappropriate, a full psychiatric and social assessment should nevertheless be carried out, and appropriate aftercare plans made, before the patient is discharged.

When the attempt has involved self-poisoning it should first be established that the young person has fully recovered from the physical effects of the overdose, otherwise confused and unreliable information may be obtained. Furthermore, the toxic effects of an overdose may prevent an adequate assessment of the individual's mental state. However, once full physical recovery is established, any delay before the assessment interview may allow defensive covering up of important facts and feelings (Connell, 1965). Interviewing of other informants, such as family members and friends, the family doctor, and any other professionals who know the person, including school teachers, can, of course, begin immediately.

Who should assess young attempted suicide patients? In many hospitals psychiatrists will take this responsibility. In some hospitals in Britain specially trained nurses, working closely with psychiatrists, have done this work (Catalan et al., 1980; Hawton, Gath, & Smith, 1979), in others, social workers have worked alongside psychiatrists (Newson-Smith & Hirsch, 1979), and in others this responsibility has been adopted by general medical teams working closely in conjunction with psychiatrists and social workers (Gardner, Hanka, O'Brien, Page, & Rees, 1977). All these schemes have been carefully evaluated and shown to be satisfactory. Because of this, the general term "assessor" will be used throughout the first half of this chapter.

Whoever takes on this responsibility in the general hospital should obtain sufficient training in order to equip themselves to make assessments and treatment arrangements with the confidence that comes from a detailed understanding of suicidal behavior, especially its reasons, motives, and consequences.

Special problems often face children and adolescents referred to hospitals after suicide attempts. These problems may also cause difficulty for an assessor. First, as noted above, some hospital staff are unsympathetic to people who have made attempts. This perhaps applies more to doctors than to nursing staff (Ramon et al., 1975). Second, young people (although this also applies to many adults) commonly feel threatened and frightened by hospital surroundings and procedures. Often it has not occurred to a person at the time of taking an overdose or inflicting a self-injury that this would result in hospital admission. Third, the person may feel ashamed and guilty about what has happened. Fourth, the assessor may be regarded as an authority figure who is in league with the individual's parents and hence not to be trusted. It is hardly surprising, therefore, that young suicide attempters often appear extremely defensive, making it difficult for any meaningful assessment to begin. Finally, immediate offers of help are commonly rejected. This may be because of the points just made. However, it should be remembered that overdoses taken by young people often appear to be intended to alter the behavior of other people rather than to obtain outside help, whatever psychiatrists and other professionals might like to believe (see Chapter 7).

In every case the assessor must consider which other informants should be interviewed. In the majority of cases these will include relatives, especially parents. Family members usually experience a confusing mixture of feelings in response to an overdose. Such feelings include sympathy, which is usually quite easily expressed, and anger and guilt, which may at first be concealed (James & Hawton, 1985). It is important that the assessor explores and facilitates ventilation of these feelings, explaining that they are common and understandable reactions.

Parents often try to trivialize their son or daughter's attempt, partly in order to avoid facing the fact that they may have failed as parents or that they have contributed to the act. Every effort should be made to help them accept that a suicide attempt is a serious event. One way of doing this, which is often effective, is to emphasize the problem-solving aspects of the behavior; in other words, to encourage them to view the overdose or self-injury as the young person's means of coping with a difficult and stressful situation.

Particular questions that should be asked of the parents are indicated below when the details of the assessment are considered. The assessor should pay careful attention to clarifying the events that led up to the act, whether there have been any noticeable changes in the person's mood or behavior of late, and whether suicide has ever been mentioned as a possibility, however remotely. Details of any history of psychiatric disorder or suicidal behavior among family members should be elicited. Finally, an assessment of the family as a whole should be made, including its dynamics, the particular role of the attempter, and the extent to which family members are supportive. Assessors of young suicide attempters should always be alert to the possibility of either child abuse or sexual abuse having contributed to the act.

Any interviews, whether with the patient or with other informants, should be conducted in privacy so that frank discussion is possible. This may be difficult when a patient must remain in bed on an open ward—it is then wise to remember that curtaining round hospital beds is not a barrier but an invitation to other patients to try to hear what is being said behind it.

Aims of the Assessment

The broad aims of the assessment of a young person who has made a suicide attempt are as follows:

   (i) to establish rapport with the person and with other informants,
  (ii) to understand the reasons for the attempt,
 (iii) to clarify the nature of the person's difficulties,
 (iv) to identify possible psychiatric disorder,
  (v) to evaluate the person's coping resources and supports, and
 (vi) to establish what help may be required.

In initiating the assessment interviews, the assessor should first try to establish a sense of rapport and trust. Above all else, the assessor should avoid appearing condemnatory. It is often best to begin by exploring the person's feelings about the act before moving on to more specific inquiry.

Details of the Assessment

The structured assessment procedure mentioned below, which is applicable with both young and adult attempters, was developed on the

TABLE 8.1
A Structured Assessment Schedule
for Use With Suicide Attempters

The assessment includes inquiry about the following areas:

(1) Events that preceded the attempt
(2) Degree of suicidal intent and other reasons for the act
(3) The individual's current problems
(4) Psychiatric disorder
(5) Family and personal history
(6) Previous psychiatric disorder or suicidal phenomena
(7) The individual's coping resources and supports
(8) Risk of a further attempt or of suicide
(9) Attitudes of the individual and family members toward further help

basis of extensive clinical experience and research investigation (Catalan et al., 1980). For further details the reader is referred elsewhere (Hawton & Catalan, 1982). The stages of the assessment are summarized in Table 8.1. The order in which the items are covered may vary between different assessors and with different patients.

(1) Events that Preceded the Attempt. A good way to begin the specific inquiry is to ask for details of the events during the few days leading up to the attempt. In addition to elucidating possible precipitants, such as a major argument or loss, this part of the assessment can provide important information concerning other items listed in Table 8.1, especially suicidal intent (for example, making specific preparation for the attempt). Absence of an obvious precipitant is more common when an attempt is the consequence of psychiatric disorder.

(2) Degree of Suicidal Intent and Other Reasons for the Act. This part of the assessment primarily relies on descriptions of the circumstances in which the attempt occurred and explanations given for the act. Information gathered from other informants as well as the attempter may be of special importance. For example, the patient may try to conceal the seriousness of intentions behind the act or vice versa. Inquiry from other people, especially concerning the circumstances of the attempt, will often reveal the true seriousness of the behavior.

Beck, Schuyler, and Herman (1974) have incorporated the main factors indicative of suicidal intent in the Beck Suicidal Intent Scale. Table 8.2 summarizes the factors concerning the circumstances of the

TABLE 8.2
Characteristics of a Suicide Attempt that
Suggest Serious Suicidal Intent

(1) Carried out in isolation
(2) Timed so that intervention unlikely
(3) Precautions taken to avoid discovery
(4) Preparations made in anticipation of death
(5) Other people informed beforehand of the individual's intention
(6) Extensive premeditation
(7) Suicide note left
(8) Failure to alert other people following the attempt

Adapted with permission from Beck et al. (1974).

attempt. In addition, the individual should be asked about his or her intention, although, as discussed earlier, the explanation may be at variance with objective evidence, and about how he or she now feels having survived the attempt. The interviewer should assess whether the individual knew of the danger (or lack of it) of the method that was used in the attempt. Although the danger involved in a self-injury may be obvious to both assessor and patient, especially where a firearm injury or jumping from a height has occurred, particular care is necessary when evaluating this aspect of overdoses. Many people who take overdoses are unaware of the likely toxicity of the substances they have swallowed. It is foolhardy and poor clinical practice to rely on the size or likely toxicity of an overdose to evaluate the person's intent (Fox & Weissman, 1975), especially if the self-poisoner has little awareness of the dangers involved (Beck, Kovacs, et al., 1975).

The evaluation of reasons for the attempt other than suicidal intent is often difficult. It will depend largely on the assessor's interpretation of the available evidence, especially concerning how the attempt relates both to the events leading up to it and to the individual's current problems. The main aim should be to evaluate the attempt in terms of problem-solving behavior, possibly using the list in Table 7.3 as a basis for this. For example, an overdose of low suicidal intent taken by a girl in front of her boyfriend following his rejection of her may well be hostile or manipulative. Minor wrist-cutting following prolonged stress may be a means of relieving tension. When an assessor feels unable to understand the behavior in this way the following three possibilities should be considered: First, that important information has been concealed or distorted; second, that crucial questions have not been asked; and, third, that the individual is suffering from a psychiatric disorder.

(3) The Individual's Current Problems. Although the nature of the attempter's problems may rapidly become obvious, it is worthwhile checking that there are not other less obvious problems. The list of problems in Table 6.1 might be used for this purpose.

(4) Psychiatric Disorder. The difficulties involved in diagnosing psychiatric disorder in young people, especially younger adolescents and children, were discussed earlier. During the interviews with the patient and with other informants, especially family members, friends, and school teachers, the assessor should be alert to the following symptoms or behaviors that may signify an underlying depression: changes in sleeping or eating habits, withdrawal from friends, unusual "acting-out behavior" (such as truancy, promiscuity, shoplifting), unsubstantiated somatic complaints, deterioration in performance at school, impaired concentration, fatigue, and irritability.

Depression in older adolescents if often similar to this disorder in adults. However, there may be potentially misleading differences. For example, there may be excessive sleeping rather than insomnia and overeating rather than loss of appetite. Uncharacteristic acting-out behavior may be another feature.

Detailed descriptions of how to assess mental state in children and adolescents can be found elsewhere (see Steinberg, 1983). In summary, the following aspects of mental state should be considered: *appearance* (facial expression, clothes, posture); *manner* and *behavior* (especially agitation or retardation, hostility, flirtation, evasion); *speech* (amount, flow, content); *mood* (especially depression and anxiety); *thought processes* (speed, structure, content); *cognitive function* (concentration, memory, orientation); *perceptual disturbances* (hallucinations); and *insight* (the patient's appraisal of any symptoms of apparent illness).

(5) Family and Personal History. This aspect of the assessment will rely to a great extent on the information from family members, rather than from the patient, especially when the latter is a child or young adolescent. The assessor should ask about any family history of

psychiatric disorder or suicidal behavior. Events in the patient's personal history that should be inquired about include his or her birth, development, and milestones; relationship with family members; sexual development and relationships (including homosexuality); relationships with peers; and school and work achievements or problems.

(6) Previous Psychiatric Disorder and Suicidal Behavior. The assessor should inquire whether the patient has a history of any psychiatric disorder, what form it took, and what treatment was provided. Evidence of previously undetected psychiatric disorder should also be sought.

If the individual has ever made a previous attempt the assessor should establish the circumstances, seriousness, and consequences of the act (or acts). It should be borne in mind that when a multiple attempter makes an attempt that is more serious than those that preceded it this may herald a fatal episode (Pierce, 1981). Questions should not only be asked about actual attempts; inquiry should also be made about suicidal thoughts or ruminations, both recent and past, and the circumstances that have provoked these.

(7) The Individual's Coping Resources and Supports. These are often difficult to assess. The patient should first be asked about previous methods of coping in the face of adversity (such as exam failure, break up of a relationship, depressive feelings). Have constructive problem-solving approaches been used, or have escapist or passive strategies been employed (such as drinking, drug use, apathy)? Second, the patient should be asked for any suggestions about how the current crisis might be solved. Third, the assessor should determine whether the individual has any supportive relationships, especially with people in whom it is possible to confide, such as a friend, family member, or professional helper, and whether such a person is currently available.

(8) Risk of a Further Attempt or of Suicide. Considerable research with adults has been devoted to identifying factors associated with risk of, first, repeat attempts and, second, suicide, but so far these have received little attention in children and adolescents. In adults, repetition is known to be associated with the following: alcohol abuse, sociopathy,

not living with relatives, previous inpatient or outpatient psychiatric treatment, previous attempts, a criminal record, and lower social class (Buglass & Horton, 1974). Although these factors may also apply to young attempters, they have not been subjected to systematic investigation. Factors that have been identified as being associated with repeats by young attempters are listed in Table 9.2. However, a word of caution is necessary: Such criteria are based upon studies of groups of subjects and may not be very helpful when assessing the risk in an individual—other less easily defined factors, such as the chances of early resolution of a current crisis, may be just as important.

Even less is known about risk factors for completed suicide in young attempters. Some of the risk factors identified for adults may well not apply (such as chronic physical disability). At present, it has only been established that the risk is greater among boys than girls, among older than younger teenagers, and among those who use potentially more dangerous methods in their attempts (Goldacre & Hawton, 1985; Otto, 1972). Clinical assessment of the particular circumstances and psychopathology of the individual is likely to provide more useful indications.

Apart from the difficulties in identifying young people at risk of further attempts or subsequent suicide, decisions about whether treatment is necessary should not be made purely on the basis of this risk. "An intervention, which is 'unnecessary' in the sense that the risk for suicide may have been low, may promote health and therefore be warranted if it succeeds in enabling patient and family to develop a more mature coping style than threat and confrontation" (Eisenberg, 1980).

(9) Attitudes of the Individual and Family Members Toward Further Help. As already noted, offers of help many initially be rejected by the young attempter. In order to assess whether any therapeutic intervention will eventually be accepted, the therapist must describe to the patient a carefully thought out therapeutic plan that is likely to be regarded by the individual as relevant to his or her problems. Lengthy therapy will often be rejected. Thus, when outpatient treatment is offered, for example, it is usually appropriate to suggest a time-limited approach with modest goals, at least in the first instance.

If family members are to be included in treatment it is essential to enlist their cooperation. Parents, unfortunately, are often keen to try to forget the whole episode and behave as if it had never happened.

THERAPY

General Aspects

It is advantageous, whenever possible, for there to be continuity of care, with the person who carried out the initial assessment also providing treatment. The major advantage is that a relationship will have been formed with the individual and his or her family at a time of crisis, which means that the therapist is both likely to have special understanding of the patient's problems and also to have a greater chance of acceptance by the patient and family members than would an unfamiliar therapist.

Therapy following a suicide attempt by a young person can often begin while the individual is still in hospital. For example, once the assessment of the individual and interviews with family members have been completed, all the family might be seen together. Although the main purpose of this is often to assess by direct observation interactions between the family members, it also offers an opportunity to begin therapy or to test out whether a family approach is indicated. Thus the therapist can observe the family's communication patterns, the degree of support between family members, their response to the attempt, and the role that the young attempter plays in the dynamics of the family.

Three major decisions must be made about future therapy: First, is treatment necessary; second, where should it occur; and, third, what form should it take?

(1) Is Treatment Necessary? Often this is a difficult question to answer. Certainly it should not be assumed that therapy is always necessary. In some cases there is no need for any further help following the assessment, and, in others, therapy will be refused. As can be seen from Table 8.3, for approximately a third of young attempters referred to the general hospital in Oxford in 1982 and 1983 following suicide attempts, no specific aftercare arrangements were made (other than informing the family doctor).

Some guidance concerning appropriate treatment can be obtained by using the classification described earlier. Adolescents in Group 1 ("acute") often appear to have problems that largely resolve as a result of the attempt. The attempt itself may appear to have been an out-of-character response to an acute stress in an otherwise normally adjusted young person. Following a thorough assessment, referral back to the care of the family doctor may be all that is necessary. In many cases, opportunity to recontact the assessor or a colleague at a time of future crisis might be offered.

Group 2 ("chronic"), the largest group in our classification scheme, contains those adolescents most likely to have symptoms of depression (although not necessarily formal psychiatric disorder), to be isolated and lonely, and to experience protracted conflict with, and lack of support from, other family members, especially their parents. This group therefore includes individuals most likely to require more active psychiatric treatment.

Group 3 ("chronic with behavior disturbance") includes young people who often engage in antisocial behavior, many of whom will currently be in contact with social or welfare agencies. Very often they already have left, or have been removed from, their families because the home environment has become too unsupportive or hostile, or the family has disintegrated. Some form of continuing care is usually necessary. Although individual treatment may be helpful, continuing intervention by social and welfare agencies is very often the most appropriate approach, with a specific emphasis on finding a supportive and emotionally warm environment in which the young person might develop.

(2) Where Should Treatment Occur? Rarely will inpatient psychiatric treatment be necessary for child and adolescent suicide attempters (Table 8.3; Hawton, Osborn, et al., 1982; White, 1974). The indications are a further need for psychiatric assessment, treatment of major psychiatric disorder, and serious risk of immediate repetition of the attempt or of suicide.

Outpatient treatment seems to be the treatment of choice in many cases (Table 8.3). When a family approach is used, treatment might be conducted in the patient's home or in an evening clinic, which may make it easier for all relevant family members to attend treatment sessions (Connell, 1965). Sometimes it will be possible to organize treatment sessions in the family doctor's health center; this may have the advantages of being closer to the family's home, hence encouraging attendance, but avoiding the possible drawbacks (such as distractions, interruptions) of home-based treatment.

TABLE 8.3
Aftercare Offered to Child and Adolescent Suicide Attempters
(Aged 12 to 20) Referred to the General Hospital in Oxford
During 1982 and 1983

	(N = 325)	
Outpatient treatment	41.5%	(7.4% of these were already receiving outpatient treatment)
Psychiatric hospital inpatient or day patient care	2.2%	(57% of these were already hospital patients)
Care of social services, child guidance, probation officer, and the like	13.5%	
Discharged to care of family doctor	41.2%	
Self-discharge before arrangements could be made	1.5%	

Of the attempters, 51.1% were also offered "open access" to the hospital psychiatric service in addition to the above aftercare arrangements.

(3) What Type of Therapy Is Indicated? The approaches that can be employed in therapy with child and adolescent suicide attempters include *family therapy, individual therapy, group therapy,* and *psychotropic medication.* Clearly these may all be used in any of the settings mentioned above. For example, during psychiatric hospital inpatient admission, a depressed adolescent might receive all four forms of therapy—individual sessions in order to further the assessment and understanding of the patient's difficulties, antidepressants to relieve depression, group therapy in order to facilitate interaction with peers, and family therapy to improve communication and support within the family and to initiate family problem-solving. In other settings, however, rarely will more than two approaches be used with any one individual.

Psychotropic drugs have only a small role in the treatment of child and adolescent suicide attempters. Antidepressants may be indicated if there is clear evidence of depression with "biological features" (loss of appetite, weight loss, insomnia), and major tranquilizers if there is evidence of a schizophrenic illness. Minor tranquilizers (such as benzodiazepines) are largely contraindicated in this group of patients because of the risks of further self-poisoning, physical and psychological dependence, withdrawal effects, and lack of evidence to indicate that they are of benefit, especially for people facing psychosocial stresses (Catalan & Gath, 1985).

Family therapy and individual therapy, which are the most important treatment approaches for child and adolescent suicide attempters, will now be considered further. However, as these are described in considerable detail elsewhere, the discussion is largely limited to specific aspects of those approaches that are important in helping people who have made suicide attempts.

Family Therapy

The importance of disturbed family interactions in the etiology of attempted suicide by young people suggests that family therapy will often be the treatment approach of choice. In practice, however, it is used less often than might be considered ideal, partly because of the lack of trained family therapists and partly because of the resistance of many families to being involved in therapy.

For detailed descriptions of family therapy in general the reader is referred to the books by Minuchin (1974) and Minuchin and Fishman (1981), and for discussion of the use of this approach with young suicide attempters, to Richman (1979). The principal aim of family therapy with suicide attempters is the modification of interactions, especially communication patterns, between family members. Further aims will include fostering support between family members and improving the family's problem-solving behavior.

The interactions upon which therapy is primarily focused may be those of the family as a whole, or those of particular subgroups: for example, a female attempter's relationship with her father, or her relationships with her siblings, or the parental relationship. However, it is important to remember that changes in the interactions between individual family members are likely to alter the dynamics of the whole family. For example, if a father begins to be more supportive of his daughter, this might have important consequences for his relationship with his wife, especially if she begins to experience jealousy about his increased attention to their daughter. It might also have implications for the interactions between the parents and their other children.

Initiation of Family Therapy

The first phase of family therapy includes an assessment by the therapist of the family structure, current transactional patterns, problem-solving skills and supports, and flexibility (that is, capacity for change). The therapist's wish to help the family must be made clear. It is also important that negative aspects of the family are not overemphasized. Thus, the strengths of the family and its individual members should be stressed.

As with all psychological therapies, at the outset the therapist should establish a clear therapeutic contract. This will include the specific goals of therapy, who will attend treatment sessions, where treatment will occur, and the proposed number and duration of sessions. A limited contract (such as six weekly sessions) is usually more likely to be accepted than a contract involving a greater commitment. Open-ended arrangements should be avoided. The therapist should bear in mind that most families are wary of psychiatric intervention and that this is a major factor predicting noncompliance (Taylor & Stansfield, 1984).

Middle Phase of Family Therapy

Once the therapist has been accepted by a family, the therapeutic approach can become more active and the family confronted with the problems that require attention.

For example, the participants could be asked to discuss between themselves an issue that has previously caused difficulty and which has remained unresolved. This provides the therapist with first-hand information about family interactions, which can then be used to point out communication patterns which require modification. Initially, the family might practice a different type of communication in the treatment session before trying it at home. Such changes might include, for example, family members paying heed to everyone else's viewpoint or ceasing to avoid discussion of difficult issues.

As therapy proceeds the focus should increasingly turn to how the family can work as a unit to tackle its problems. The therapist may have to reframe the nature of problems for the family in order to increase the chance of problem-solving strategies being found. For example, a problem such as "she (daughter) never tells us (parents) anything" might be reframed by a therapist into "why does she find it so difficult to confide in us?" or "what can we do to make it easier for her?"

Gradually the family should be encouraged to regain its autonomy, with the individual members taking full responsibility for their actions and being required to work out their own solutions to problems. Failure of a family to do this may herald a poor outcome.

Discussions about therapy with suicide attempters often neglect a very important aspect of treatment, namely the attempt itself. Usually, it is essential to explore the meaning of the attempt to individual family members, and especially to identify differences between their explanations. For example, a father may regard his daughter's overdose as a childish means of trying to change his mind about something, while she regards it as the only way in which she could escape from an intolerable conflict situation and make her parents aware of how distressed she was feeling. Such a discrepancy, unless explored and resolved, might have long-standing consequences for the father's attitude toward his daughter. It might also increase the chances of a repeat attempt. During such exploration the therapist must first emphasize that the behavior is to be regarded as serious, even if death was not intended, because it was a drastic last-ditch attempt to deal with an intolerable situation. The aim should not necessarily be to get one person to change his or her explanation for the overdose but rather to help both individuals recognize and accept each other's interpretation of the behavior, and then to discuss how in future such a situation might be prevented or resolved.

Termination of Family Therapy

Intervals between the final few sessions of therapy might be longer than between earlier sessions in order to allow more time for the family members to consolidate their progress while still receiving the support of the therapist. One follow-up session, two or three months after the end of treatment, will allow the therapist to reassess the family's progress and to discuss any further difficulties that have occurred.

Limitations of Family Therapy

By no means are all young suicide attempters suited to family therapy. In many cases the family will be either physically or psychologically unavailable. The older adolescent attempter, for example, may already have separated from his or her family, or the family may have disintegrated. A common contraindication is lack of motivation of family members. Sometimes a combined approach of both family and individual sessions is useful, especially if a young person has difficulties outside as well as inside the family, or where issues of confidentiality are posed by family therapy.

Individual Therapy

In addition to the indications for individual therapy noted above, it will also often be indicated with older adolescents, whose problems may include, for example, difficulty coping with a loss, social isolation, and feelings of hopelessness concerning the future. For wrist-cutters, individual therapy is often the treatment of choice.

Brief Problem-Solving Therapy (Crisis Intervention)

Individual therapy is often based on the principles of crisis intervention (Bartolucci & Drayer, 1973). Thus therapy will usually be brief (between one and ten sessions), intensive (lasting just a few weeks, but with very short intervals between the early sessions), focused on current problems, and with the principal aims of obtaining resolution of the current crisis and the adoption of more adaptive coping methods in future. Since this approach is described in detail elsewhere (see Ewing, 1978; Hawton & Catalan, 1982), only brief mention will be made of the main components and those aspects particularly relevant to young suicide attempters.

Briefly, in crisis or problem-solving therapy, the therapist tries to form a supportive relationship with the patient that will allow them to work together in a collaborative fashion in order to solve the patient's problems. The suicidal adolescent often lacks a sense of control over his or her environment and future. Helping reestablish a sense of autonomy is often a crucial first step in therapy.

Initially the therapist tries to help the patient to clarify, in precise detail, the nature of the problems that must be tackled. Target problems are usually of two types—a choice between alternatives (for example, "should I stay in my current job or should I try something else?") and attainment of specific goals (for instance, "How can I meet more friends?" "How can I cope with the loss of my boyfriend?").

Once a problem has been clarified, the therapist then assists the patient to work out what steps need to be taken in order to begin to solve the problem. Usually the initial steps should be small (for example, writing a list of pros and cons about alternative courses of action). The patient is encouraged to try to carry out the initial step before the next therapy session. The therapist's role at the subsequent session is to explore what happened. If the patient has successfully carried out the first step, then the next should be tried. If failure has been experienced, the therapist must help the patient explore the reasons for this (fear of the consequences, for example), and then encourage the patient to try again using the same approach or to try an alternative approach to the problem.

Techniques employed in cognitive therapy with depressed adults (Beck, Rush, Shaw, & Emery, 1979) may also be useful in helping adolescent suicide attempters. Thus the therapist might assist the patient to recognize and reappraise negative cognitions that are posing a barrier to constructive action. This may facilitate problem-solving, as well as helping relieve depressive feelings.

Other therapeutic strategies that can usefully be incorporated in crisis or problem-solving therapy include specific advice, contracting, provision of information, referral to other specialist agencies, and, very occasionally, prescription of psychotropic drugs (see Hawton & Catalan, 1982, for details of these strategies).

Longer term psychotherapy may be indicated for adolescents with severe intrapsychic difficulties, especially when these are interfering with an individual's ability to form relationships. Brief problem-solving therapy is often a useful prelude to long-term psychotherapy, as it can help establish whether the latter is necessary, and will allow further evaluation of the adolescent's motivation and "psychological mindedness."

Preventive Measures

It is important, as noted above, not to neglect the actual event that led to therapy in the first place—the suicide attempt itself. Often it is preferable to leave exploration of the possible motives behind the attempt until the patient's problems are beginning to resolve. There may be greater willingness at that stage to consider, for example, that the act may have included hostile or manipulative motives. Once the reasons for the behavior have been clarified, ways of preventing a further attempt at a time of crisis should be explored. The patient might, for example, rehearse in imagination how a subsequent crisis could be dealt with. Some patients are helped by having a telephone number that will allow them to seek assistance from the therapist or a colleague ("open access" or "hotline") if a further crisis arises. Simply knowing that such help is available if absolutely necessary may be sufficient to allow a person to face adversity successfully; in other cases the open access facility will be used to get further help.

Play Therapy

Often children will not respond to direct exploration of their difficulties. Then it is usually helpful to use one of their natural methods of exploration, namely, play. Construction of scenes using plasticine models or paintings may provide information that can help the therapist develop a fuller understanding of what is troubling the patient, although the inferences that may be made must be tentative.

Individual Therapy with Self-Cutters

Individuals who indulge in minor self-cutting, especially those who repeatedly cut themselves, are often difficult to help. An appropriate therapeutic approach to their general problems (such as individual problem-solving therapy, family therapy, or psychiatric hospital in-patient care) should be chosen according to the indications that have already been discussed. However, specific measures might also be tried in order to modify and eliminate the self-cutting itself. Since this behavior is often related to intolerable feelings of tension that are relieved by cutting, such measures are primarily concerned with tension reduction.

First, the therapist should help the patient establish the common precipitants of the feelings that precede self-cutting, and then explore coping strategies that might help prevent these feelings developing in the first place. Self-relaxation, as used in systematic desensitization, may prove helpful. Rehearsing counter thoughts to tension-provoking thoughts is another possible measure. In order to discharge feelings of tension once they have begun to mount up, vigorous exercise may prove beneficial, especially as this usually leads to a sense of relaxation. It may also be helpful to suggest that the patient wears a rubber band around the wrist that can be flicked to elicit mild pain (but no skin damage) when tension occurs. Repeatedly squeezing a rubber ball in the hand until there is considerable discomfort in the wrist and forearm has also been described in the management of wrist cutters (Rosen & Thomas, 1984).

Compliance with Outpatient Therapy

Attendance by young suicide attempters at outpatient sessions is often poor. Initial nonattendance rates of between 21% (White, 1974) and 44% (Taylor & Stansfield, 1984) have been reported. Litt, Cuskey, and Rudd (1983) found that as many as 61% of adolescent suicide attempters seen in an emergency room in a hospital in California failed to complete the aftercare recommendations. However, in this case it appeared that the aftercare was usually arranged with someone other than the original assessor, a factor likely to increase noncompliance.

Taylor and Stansfield (1984) found that attendance of adolescent self-poisoners at outpatient treatment sessions was more likely if an adolescent had (1) severe psychological symptoms, especially those of depression, loss of appetite, and insomnia; (2) a definite psychiatric disorder; (3) taken the overdose in response to family arguments; (4) taken the overdose with suicidal intent; and (5) parents with positive attitudes toward psychiatric treatment. A further discriminating factor between attenders and nonattenders in the study by Litt and colleagues (1983) was a history of previous attempts. In fact, in their study none of those who had made previous attempts complied with the emergency room follow-up recommendations.

In order to enhance the likelihood of establishing an effective therapeutic alliance with young suicide attempters, special attention needs to be paid to (1) continuity of care; (2) ensuring that treatment is viewed as relevant to the real needs of the individual; (3) keeping intervention as brief as possible; (4) dealing with here-and-now issues (at least initially); and (5) tailoring the schedule and timing of therapy sessions to the patient's circumstances—a rigid once-weekly regime is unlikely to be as helpful as flexible timing of sessions according to need.

CONCLUSIONS

The management of child and adolescent suicide attempters involves complex issues. This chapter has provided a summary of the important aspects of management and highlighted some of the problems and ways of overcoming these. Treatment should not be undertaken until a full assessment has been carried out. In addition to the usual aims of a psychiatric assessment, it is important to try to develop some understanding of the actual attempt, especially the degree of suicidal intent, and to assess the risks of a further attempt and of suicide. Although risk factors for repeat attempts and for suicide have been suggested, these do not provide a sufficient basis for judgment in the individual case. The particular circumstances and psychopathology of the individual are likely to provide a better guide.

Subsequent treatment must be carefully tailored to the patient's needs. Family therapy is often indicated (although less often feasible) for child and young adolescent attempters. Individual therapy is the treatment of choice for many older adolescents, especially if their problems lie outside the family, or other family members are unwilling or unable to be involved in treatment.

Treatment is usually best organized using the principles of crisis intervention. Thus it should be brief, focused on clear goals, concerned largely with here-and-now issues, and directed toward improving the patient's problem-solving skills. Longer term therapy, or inpatient psychiatric care, is rarely necessary, and psychotropic drugs have little place in therapy, except in adolescents with psychiatric disorders.

Compliance with aftercare may be poor unless there is continuity of care, flexibility in the therapy schedule, and the focus of treatment appears realistic and relevant to the individual patient.

9

OUTCOME FOLLOWING ATTEMPTED SUICIDE

In view of the general concern about suicidal acts by children and adolescents it comes as a surprise to find that there have been few studies examining either the short-term or long-term outcome for young people making suicide attempts. This chapter will therefore focus on outcome, particularly in terms of (1) social and psychological adjustment; (2) further suicide attempts; and (3) completed suicide.

One reason for the relative paucity of outcome studies is that they involve problematical methodological issues. A major difficulty in assessing adjustment, especially if there is a long delay between the initial attempt and the follow-up, is that the subjects may not wish to be interviewed (Nardini-Maillard & Ladame, 1980); often this may be because individuals do not wish to be reminded of the act. It was for this reason that Otto (1972) abandoned an interview-based follow-up study in Sweden, and instead relied on medical and social records to provide information about outcome. Some research workers have tried using postal questionnaires for follow-up but have encountered extremely low response rates. For example, of 235 questionnaires sent to adolescent suicide attempters and control subjects by Mehr, Zeltzer, and Robinson (1982) only 12.3% were returned. Obviously, findings from such an inquiry are likely to be highly misleading because the subjects who reply may differ in important respects from those who do not.

When studying repetition of attempts it is usual to identify individuals who re-present at hospitals within a given geographical area. Account should be taken of the high mobility among suicide attempters, especially repeaters, which will mean that some at-risk subjects may have moved away from the area. Thus their further attempts will not be identified by this method.

Information about suicidal deaths following attempted suicide is usually more complete, in that most countries maintain a register of suicides. However, all the factors influencing the identification of suicides, which were discussed earlier in this book, are likely to affect the findings.

SOCIAL AND PSYCHOLOGICAL ADJUSTMENT

In examining the subsequent adjustment of adolescents who make suicide attempts, three studies will be reviewed in which the subjects were followed up for different periods of time: first, the author and colleagues' study in Oxford in which adolescent self-poisoners were followed up one month after their overdoses (Hawton, Cole, et al., 1982; Hawton, Osborn, et al., 1982); second, White's (1974) study in Birmingham, England, in which adolescents who took overdoses were followed up one year later; and third, a much longer term follow-up (10 to 15 years after the attempts) in Sweden, reported by Otto (1972).

All 50 adolescent self-poisoners in the Oxford study (Chapter 6) were interviewed one month after their overdoses. This unusually high follow-up rate reflected the relatively short follow-up period and the fact that the research interviewers obtained considerable information during the initial interviews about how to recontact the adolescents. Using a global rating of outcome, by comparison with general adjustment at the time of the overdose, the research interviewers rated 33 (66%) of the adolescents as "improved," 16 (32%) as "unchanged," and one as "worse." Problems that most often tended to have improved during the month following the overdoses were those concerning boyfriends and girlfriends (the relationships often having finally ceased), alcohol, peers, and finance. Problems with parents were only improved in half the adolescents who had such difficulties at the time of the overdose. When the adolescents were asked whether the overdose had produced any positive changes in their problems, half the subjects said that it had, 42% said that it had not, and 8% were unsure.

When outcome, in terms of overall adjustment, was examined in the context of the classification scheme that was described earlier, a clear difference was found between the three groups (Table 9.1). Thus 90% of subjects in the acute group were rated as "improved," compared with

TABLE 9.1
Short-Term Outcome and Repetition of Attempts
in 50 Adolescent Self-Poisoners

Group*	Improved Overall Adjustment 1 Month After the Overdose (N)	Repeat Attempts During Year Following the Overdose (N)
(1) Acute (N = 10)	90% (9)	10% (1)
(2) Chronic (N = 28)	75% (21)	0% (0)
(3) Chronic with behavior disturbance (N = 12)	25% (3)	50% (6)
	x^2 = 12.57 p < .01	Group 3 versus Groups 1 and 2 x^2 = 13.29 p < .001

*Method of classification described in Chapter 6.

75% in the chronic group and only 25% in the chronic group with behavior disturbance.

This study demonstrated that the short-term outcome for the majority of adolescent self-poisoners is relatively good. However, approximately one-third of the adolescents in this study were still facing serious difficulties four weeks after their overdoses; these were individuals who, at the time of the overdose, were most likely to have had problems lasting more than one month and also to have shown disturbed behavior.

White (1974) was able to follow up 40 out of 50 adolescent self-poisoners (aged 13 to 19 years) one year after their overdoses. It is not entirely clear from his report how the follow-up inquiry was conducted. Twenty-eight subjects (56%) were rated as improved at follow-up, and 12 (24%) had either experienced no change or they were worse. The ten subjects (20%) who were not available for follow-up had either changed their address or were not known to their family doctors. White suggested that they comprised an unstable group and were unlikely to have shown less morbidity than those who were available for follow-up. He concluded that at least a quarter of adolescent self-poisoners are still experiencing considerable difficulties a year after their overdoses.

Otto (1972) followed up 1547 adolescent suicide attempters in Sweden 10 to 15 years after their attempts, using the standardized medical and social records that are available in that country. Compared with an age, sex, and nationality-matched control group, the overall death rate during the follow-up period was three times higher among the suicide attempters, the difference being greater among the boys. The suicide attempters of both sexes had a significantly lower rate of marriage and a higher rate of divorce than the controls. Emigration from Sweden, preventive detention, entry in the criminal register, imprisonment, probation orders, and sick leave for either psychiatric or physical reasons had all occurred more frequently among the suicide attempters. In general, more of the boys than the girls had shown evidence of mental ill health during the follow-up period.

REPETITION OF SUICIDE ATTEMPTS

Repetition of attempted suicide can first be considered by examining evidence about the proportion of young suicide attempters who have made attempts resulting in hospital referral *prior* to an index attempt. This proportion has varied considerably between different studies: for example, 12% (Hawton, Cole, et al., 1982); 14% (White, 1974); 18% (Rohn, Sarles, Kenny, Reynolds, & Head, 1977); 22% (Headlam et al., 1979); and 40% (Mattsson et al., 1969). Thus, very approximately, about a quarter of adolescent suicide attempters will have a history of at least one previous attempt. Not surprisingly, given the shorter time that adolescents will have been at risk, this is a smaller proportion than is found among adult attempters. For example, Bancroft and Marsack (1977) identified previous attempts in 36% of a large series of adult attempters referred to a general hospital. However, adolescents not uncommonly report minor self-injuries and overdoses that have not come to medical attention. For example, in the Oxford study a further 18% of the adolescents (in addition to the 12% who had come to medical attention) reported episodes of this kind (Hawton, Cole, et al., 1982).

Follow-up studies of small samples of adolescent suicide attempters have suggested that approximately one in ten will make a further attempt leading to hospital referral during the year after an attempt (Haldane & Haider, 1967; Hawton, Cole, et al., 1982). Again this is a lower repetition rate than in adult attempters, among whom rates of 15 to 25% have been reported (Bancroft & Marsack, 1977; Kreitman, 1977; Morgan, 1979). As might be expected, much higher repetition rates are found in adolescent suicide attempters who have been admitted to psychiatric in-patient care; for example, Barter and associates (1968) reported a rate of 42% during a 22-month follow-up period for such a sample.

Repetition among a very large group of adolescent attempters has been studied by Goldacre and Hawton (1985) who used record-linked hospital data to study repetition by 2492 self-poisoners aged 12 to 20 years in the Oxford region in the United Kingdom. Altogether, 6.3% repeated within one year of their first admission during the study period. This figure must have been a slight underestimate because it was only based on hospital *admissions* (not referrals) and did not include repeats that occurred outside the Oxford region. The highest repetition rates for each sex were seen at the ages at which admission rates for self-poisoning showed the sharpest rise, namely in the early teenage years for girls and in the older teenage years for boys (Hawton & Goldacre, 1982). Repetition rates were significantly higher among boys than girls in the 16 to 20 age group. The greatest risk of a repeat was during the first few months after an attempt, a similar picture to that reported for adults (Bancroft & Marsack, 1977). This presumably reflects persistence, or early recurrence, of the crisis that precipitated the first overdose.

The characteristics that distinguish repeaters from nonrepeaters have been examined in several studies. However, scales that might aid the clinician to detect likely repeaters have not been developed for adolescents. A study is required that identifies factors that appear to distinguish repeaters from nonrepeaters in one cohort, then reduces the number of factors by some statistical method such as multiple regression analysis, and finally validates these factors in a prospective study, preferably of more than one cohort of subjects. This kind of investigation has been carried out among adults (Buglass & Horton, 1974; Buglass & McCulloch, 1970), but not among adolescents. Only Choquet and colleagues (1980) in France have made any progress in the development of a predictive scale for adolescents.

Table 9.2 summarizes the findings of several studies in which characteristics distinguishing repeaters from nonrepeaters have been reported (Choquet et al., 1980; Goldacre & Hawton, 1985; Hawton, Cole, et al., 1982; Hawton, Osborn, et al., 1982; Headlam et al., 1979; Stanley & Barter, 1970). There is obviously considerable overlap between items on this list. Choquet and associates (1980) found a particularly high risk of repetition among individuals in whom psychiatric or personality disorders were associated with at least three out of five other factors (4, 5, 6, 11, and 12 in Table 9.2).

Other factors likely to predict risk of immediate repetition are the extent to which the young person's problems appear to have altered as a

TABLE 9.2

**Characteristics Probably Associated with Increased Risk
of Repeat Attempts by Adolescent Suicide Attempters**

(1)	Male sex, especially among older teenagers
(2)	Previous attempts
(3)	Psychiatric/personality disorder
(4)	Coming from a large family
(5)	Alcoholism in family
(6)	Disturbed relationships with family members
(7)	Not living with parents
(8)	Chronic problems and behavior disturbance
(9)	Alcohol/drug abuse
(10)	Social isolation
(11)	Poor school record
(12)	Depressive tendencies

result of the attempt and the availability of supports. These factors are largely assessed by clinical judgment and as such are difficult to quantify.

EVENTUAL COMPLETED SUICIDE

Eventual death by suicide among child and adolescent attempters has been investigated rarely. The longest follow-up study appears to have been Otto's (1972) Swedish investigation, which was described earlier. Of 1547 subjects aged 10 to 20 years, 84 died during the 10 to 15 year follow-up period, in 67 cases (80%) by suicide. The proportion committing suicide (4.3% of the total sample) was far higher among the boys (10%) than the girls (2.9%). The suicide rate was highest during the first two years of follow-up. Although boys were at greatest risk of suicide, girls who had made active attempts (such as hanging) were at greater risk of subsequent suicide than those who had used passive means (such as drugs). The suicide rate in this study was not much less than that reported for adult attempters (Kreitman, 1977).

In the United Kingdom, Goldacre and Hawton (1985) found six probable suicides (only one of whom had officially been reported as such) out of ten deaths among 2492 adolescent self-poisoners aged 12 to 20 years who were followed-up for an average of 2.8 years. Four of the suicides were among boys aged 19 or 20 years at the time of their original overdoses, the other two being girls aged 18 at the time of the original overdoses. Therefore, the risk of eventual suicide is probably greater among older than younger adolescent suicide attempters, as well as being more common among boys than girls.

The discrepancy between the rates of suicide found in these two studies (4.3% over 10 to 15 years in Otto's and 0.24% over a mean of 2.8 years reported in Goldacre and Hawton's) probably results from at least two factors. First, the Swedish study included adolescents who injured themselves as well as those who took overdoses, the suicide rate being higher in the former group. Second, the adolescents in the Swedish study had made their original attempts between 1955 and 1959, those in the English study between 1974 and 1977. In between these two studies there was a vast increase in the incidence of attempted suicide, and this was probably the result of a disproportionate increase in the number of adolescents making less serious attempts, who, in turn, are less likely eventually to commit suicide. Nevertheless, a significant number of deaths by suicide still occur among adolescent attempters, and this remains a cause for considerable concern.

CONCLUSIONS

For the majority of adolescent suicide attempters, the outcome following attempts is relatively good, with improved adjustment occurring in many cases within a month of the attempt. However, a substantial minority of such adolescents continue to have major difficulties following their attempts, as evidenced by high rates of psychiatric and physical disorder, poor marital adjustment, and elevated rates of criminality, as well as repeat attempts.

Several predictive factors appear to be associated with increased risk of subsequent repetition of attempted suicide among adolescent attempters, including extensive family psychopathology, poor social and psychological adjustment, and having made a previous attempt. The risk of repetition seems to be highest among older teenage boys.

The long-term risk of suicide among adolescent attempters is significant. Boys who make attempts are at particular risk of subsequently taking their own lives. Further work is required to determine other risk factors.

10

PREVENTION OF CHILD AND ADOLESCENT SUICIDAL BEHAVIOR

With the recent increase in both attempted and completed suicide, the need to find effective means of preventing suicidal behavior among young people has become more pressing. In considering possible measures, primary prevention must be distinguished from secondary prevention. The principal aim of *primary prevention* is prevention of any suicidal acts in the first place, whereas that of *secondary prevention* is prevention of further suicidal behavior once an individual has made an attempt.

PRIMARY PREVENTION

Several suggestions have been made concerning the primary prevention of suicidal behavior in young people (see "Children and parasuicide," 1981), based mostly on the premise that suicidal behavior would be less likely if social and psychological welfare were improved. However, there appears to have been little in the way of implementation of these suggestions, and even less in the way of evaluation. Some broad measures that have been suggested include social support to poorly functioning families; improvement in the diagnosis and treatment of depression and other psychiatric disorders in childhood; an increase in educational programs in child and adolescent psychiatry for family doctors and hospital and community physicians; and courses aimed at helping parents, teachers, and social workers become more aware of the problems of young people.

A more specific suggestion has been that schools should devote a significant portion of their curricula to problem-solving skills for when pupils face difficult life situations. Discussion of coping skills might include examination of maladaptive methods, including suicidal acts, as well as more adaptive methods. The use of currently available helping agencies might be encouraged for those who feel overwhelmed by their difficulties. Some schools have already introduced this approach.

Contacts with Potential Helping Agencies

One important aspect of possible prevention concerns the contacts that young people have had with potential helping agencies before their attempts. It is well known that the majority of adults who either attempt suicide (Hawton & Blackstock, 1976) or actually kill themselves (Barraclough et al., 1974) have seen their family doctors during the month before these acts. In addition, some will have been in contact with other potential helpers, such as social workers, psychiatrists, clergymen, and volunteers in suicide prevention agencies (Bancroft, Skrimshire, Casson, Harvard-Watts, & Reynolds, 1977). Similar frequencies of contacts with helping agencies appear to precede adolescent suicide attempts. In Oxford, for example, it was found that half of a series of adolescent self-poisoners had consulted their family doctor within one month of the overdose, and about a quarter within one week. There was, however, a marked age difference in that the proportion of older adolescents (16 to 18 years) who had seen their doctors was similar to that found for adult attempters, whereas far fewer of the younger adolescents (13 to 15 years) had recently contacted their doctors (Hawton, Cole, et al., 1982). Hence there is less possibility of prevention through such contacts for younger adolescents. Smaller proportions of these adolescent self-poisoners had been in contact with either social work (24%) or psychiatric agencies (12%) within the month prior to their overdose.

The next question therefore is how feasible is it for family doctors to detect those at risk of suicidal behavior? The major problem is that the criteria that might be used are very crude and would apply to a vast number of people who will not carry out suicidal acts as well as those who will. In other words, the rate of false positive identification would be far too high to base detection of those at risk entirely on such factors. The risk factors for attempted suicide will be obvious from Chapters 5 and 6. For example, girls are more at risk than boys; the risk during adolescence increases with age; those at particular risk are likely to have a history of a broken home or poor relationships with their parents; to have a family history of psychiatric disorder and/or suicidal behaviors; and to have been a victim of child (and possibly sexual) abuse. Current stresses might include conflict with parents, the break-up of a close relationship, school or work difficulties (including unemployment), social isolation, and minor physical ailments. It can be seen that such criteria will apply to many adolescents. However, when these are a background to depressive symptomatology the risk will be increased. In such individuals it is suggested that special inquiry should be made to explore possible suicidal ideas, including concrete plans for a suicidal act.

Risk factors for suicide are even less precise. We know that boys are more likely to kill themselves than girls and that suicide is very rare under the age of 14. Shaffer (1974) has suggested that the following risk factors for younger adolescents are worth noting: intellectual and physical precocity, previous suicidal behavior, and a broken home or loss of a parent. In an adolescent rendered "at risk" by these background factors, an acute interpersonal or social crisis may increase the chance of suicide. Shaffer suggested that the most commonly occurring precedent was a situation in which the adolescent knew that his or her parents were about to be told of some misdemeanor or loss of face outside the home. Disputes with peers and with boy or girlfriends were also found to precede suicide. Furthermore, Shaffer noted that many suicides took place after a period of absence from school, a phenomenon that has also been noted in studies of attempted suicide (Stanley & Barter, 1970).

In older adolescents, further risk factors may include unemployment, alcoholism and drug addiction, as well as, of course, other serious psychiatric disorders, especially depression and schizophrenia (particularly in its early stages).

In young people it is generally wise to take seriously any threats of suicide, however vaguely couched. Such ideas should be acknowledged, not condemned or pushed aside. When depression or suicidal ideas are accompanied by a sense of hopelessness this is a particularly important warning sign. Obviously the individual's history and circumstances should be adequately explored. Once a young person at risk has been identified what should then be done? The most important step may be to ensure that the young person has a constant supportive figure who can be trusted and who is available throughout the period of greatest stress.

Family doctors may feel able to play this role in some cases. In other cases referral to a counseling service for young people (of which there are an increasing number), or to a child or adolescent psychiatry service may be necessary.

It must be remembered that depression in children and adolescents is, by comparison with affective disorder in adults, very often atypical. It is likely to be heavily colored by the individual's stage of development. In children, psychosomatic complaints may be the primary manifestations; in adolescents, psychiatric symptoms, withdrawal, and behavioral disturbances are more likely. Diagnosis is probably best made by a specialist in child or adolescent psychiatry. Although antidepressant therapy may be indicated, in the majority of cases it will be apparent that social and interpersonal factors must be the main focus of treatment.

Reduced Availability of Medication and Other Means of Suicide

Since the means employed in suicidal acts (medication, guns, ropes, knives, high buildings, automobiles) are so readily available it may appear pointless to suggest that reducing their availability would help prevent the behavior. However, as Eisenberg (1980) has noted: (1) many suicidal acts are impulsive and rely on the immediate availability of a method; (2) even in those with serious suicidal intent, one method may be acceptable while others are not; and (3) many suicide attempters are highly ambivalent about going through with an attempt.

It has been suggested that more cautious prescribing of psychotropic drugs for young people may prevent overdoses ("Children and para-suicide," 1981; Morgan, 1979; White, 1974). While the author concurs with this suggestion, the reader is reminded that young adolescents often take overdoses of nonprescribed drugs. Would, therefore, reducing the availability of nonprescribed drugs also help? Limiting the quantities of analgesic preparations available over the counter in chemist shops (drug stores) is an obvious measure, and another is to increase the alertness of assistants in such shops to detect individuals who appear distressed. The use of special blister packaging of tablets, or wrapping tablets individually in foil to delay ingestion when an overdose is impulsive, have also been suggested (Fox, 1975).

Most households contain several varieties of medicines, few of which are used regularly. In view of the impulsiveness of many overdoses by young people, educating people to keep only the most limited supply of medicines, and to ensure that these are kept in a secure place, might help prevent a few overdoses.

In places such as the United States where firearms are increasingly used for suicide, it is likely that gun control legislation would help prevent a considerable number of suicidal deaths. While use of a gun may appear to imply very serious suicidal intent, even in such cases ambivalence about living or dying is common.

Media Reporting of Suicides

As discussed earlier, there is considerable evidence to suggest that publicity concerning individual suicides may facilitate such behavior in other people. There are good grounds therefore for questioning the way in which suicides are reported in the media and even whether they should be reported at all. Although it is unlikely that reporting of suicides would ever cease, and there are arguments in favor of saying it should not, extensive reporting of suicides should be discouraged.

Suicide Prevention Agencies

In Britain the Samaritan organization was introduced by Chad Varah in 1953 with the aim of befriending people who were desperate or suicidal. Since that time this organization has grown extensively. There was considerable enthusiasm for suicide prevention and crisis intervention centers in the United States during the 1960s and early 1970s. Furthermore, agencies specializing in providing help for adolescents have also appeared. Most suicide prevention agencies have a 24-hour telephone service, manned by volunteers, and can provide confidential counseling. Some have close links with psychiatric agencies.

The enthusiasm of many people for such centers has been matched by skepticism on the part of others. Particular controversy has surrounded the question of whether they actually prevent suicides to any significant degree. In Britain, Bagley (1968) reported evidence of a decline in suicide rates in cities in which branches of the Samaritans had been established and an increase in matched cities which did not have Samaritan branches. However, a replication of this study, which included control cities which the authors claimed were better matched than those in Bagley's study, failed to support Bagley's finding (Jennings, Barraclough, & Moss, 1978). This was followed by considerable debate in the literature, which included a different analysis of the data of Jennings and colleagues suggesting their conclusions were incorrect (Innes, 1980). Current opinion is that there is no convincing evidence either way as to the effectiveness of the suicide prevention role of the Samaritans.

Two investigations of suicide prevention centers in the United States failed to demonstrate any substantial preventive effect (Weiner, 1969; Lester, 1974). A recent study, however, has been more encouraging, especially with regard to preventing suicides by young people (Miller, Coombs, Leeper, & Barton, 1984). The suicide rates in the United States in counties in which crisis intervention centers were established between 1968 and 1973 were compared with those of counties in which such centers were not available during this period. Little overall change in suicide rates occurred across all the counties. For young white females (0 to 24 years), however, there was a significant difference between the two types of counties, with a decline in rates in counties in which crisis centers were established (–55%) and an increase in those in which they were not (+85%). This finding was replicated in a different set of counties for a different time span. The credibility of this finding is increased by the knowledge that young white females are by far the most frequent callers to crisis or suicide prevention centers. The authors estimated that more than 600 lives per year might be saved by universal availability of suicide prevention centers throughout the United States.

SECONDARY PREVENTION

As noted at the beginning of this chapter, the aim of secondary prevention is the prevention of further episodes of suicidal behavior, either further attempts or fatal episodes. However, this concept should be extended to include the improvement of patients' social and psychological difficulties. While this may help prevent further suicidal acts, it should also be a goal by itself.

Prevention of Further Attempts

Probable risk factors for further attempts by young people are listed in Table 9.2. It might be argued that, for secondary prevention to succeed, intervention should be focused primarily on young people with these characteristics. There is of course considerable sense behind this argument. However, two problems should be borne in mind. First, many of these characteristics are also those that are associated with poor compliance with aftercare. Second, many individuals with such characteristics will not make further attempts. As was noted in the previous chapter, other very important factors to take into account are the chances of a person's current crisis resolving very soon and the degree of support available.

So far there have been no reports of properly controlled research studies of intervention aimed at reducing repetition of attempts by young people. Efforts to reduce repetition among adult attempters have not been encouraging. In the United Kingdom, for example, intensive aftercare did not have any impact on repetition among multiple repeaters studied in Edinburgh (Chowdhury, Hicks, & Kreitman, 1973), well-organized social work aftercare did not affect repetition among suicide attempters in Southampton (Gibbons, Butler, Urwin, & Gibbons, 1978), and home-based treatment of self-poisoners did not make any difference to repetition rates by comparison with outpatient treatment, in spite of better compliance with the domiciliary approach (Hawton, Brancroft, et al., 1981). Intensive treatment programs using behavioral approaches (such as anxiety management, social skills training, family contractual therapy) with repeat attempters have produced some slightly more encouraging results (Kass, Silvers, & Abroms, 1972; Liberman & Eckman, 1981) but have not yet been subjected to adequate evaluation.

It is quite possible, of course, that prevention of repeat attempts by children and adolescents might be easier than with adults because of the greater potential for psychological development among young people. However, this suggestion needs empirical support.

Prevention of Suicide

The paucity of indicators of eventual suicide by young attempters was noted in Chapter 9. Older boys, individuals who use violent methods in their attempts, those whose attempts have involved serious suicidal intent, and those with major psychiatric disorders (especially depression and schizophrenia) are probably most at risk. Alcoholism and drug addiction are likely to be further risk factors. However, the problems of using similarly crude criteria in the prediction of suicide by adult attempters have been fully expounded by Kreitman (1982). The main difficulty stems from the low base rate of suicide, even among those at greatest risk, and the poor sensitivity and specificity of the predictive factors. Thus, while it might be possible to delineate a group of individuals that would include most of those who would eventually kill themselves, the size of this group would be so large that intensive intervention would not be feasible. As the base rate of suicide is even lower and the risk factors cruder for young suicide attempters by comparison with adults, this problem is further compounded in this age group.

These problems should not of course mean that all efforts at suicide prevention are abandoned. Intensive therapy, including inpatient psychiatric hospital treatment where indicated, should be provided for individuals who have made serious attempts and those suffering from major depressive or psychotic disorders. Treatment with antidepressants or major tranquilizers may be necessary in such cases. After completion of intensive therapy, there should be careful follow-up, with vigilance by doctors, other professionals, and family members, for early signs of recurrence of the condition that led to the attempt. The greatest risk of suicide is during the weeks or months following an attempt—it should be feasible to prevent many such deaths by arranging properly organized aftercare. Prevention in the longer term may be less easy. In addition to preventing the deaths of some individuals, active aftercare programs are very likely to improve the social circumstances and psychological well-being of considerably more.

Amelioration of Social and Psychological Problems

While there is little evidence that treatment programs have much impact on repetition rates of adult suicide attempters, it appears that they are of rather more benefit in terms of psychosocial functioning. For example, the treatment program for chronic repeaters in Edinburgh resulted in more improvement in social problems, especially for the women, than did conventional care (Chowdhury et al., 1973), and the subjects who received social work care in the Southampton study reported greater improvement in their social circumstances than did those for whom special aftercare was not available (Gibbons et al., 1978). Investigation is now required to determine what types of intervention might be of special benefit to child and adolescent suicide attempters. This would presumably include family and individual counseling where appropriate. It would also be useful to know who is most likely to benefit from such help.

CONCLUSIONS

Prevention of child and adolescent suicidal behavior has been considered with regard to primary and secondary prevention. Although it is possible to delineate characteristics of young people at risk of suicidal acts, these characteristics will also apply to many individuals who will not engage in such behavior. This is a recurring problem in suicide prevention generally. Although doctors, other health professionals, and teachers should be vigilant for young people who are under stress, especially if they show characteristics known to be common among suicidal individuals, prevention is perhaps best considered as part of a wider approach to helping equip young people with coping skills. This is why the introduction into school curricula of sessions in which problem-solving is discussed is so attractive. Reducing the availability of dangerous means of suicidal behavior should be given serious consideration, remembering that many suicidal acts are associated with considerable ambivalence and that while one method may be attractive to a person, others may not. The way in which suicides are reported in the media should be reappraised, especially in the light of considerable evidence that this may facilitate suicidal acts by other people.

While it is likely that suicide prevention centers may offer considerable help for distressed and lonely individuals, doubt surrounds their efficacy in actually preventing suicides. There has, however, been an encouraging recent report from the United States suggesting that these centers may have a particular role in preventing suicides of young women.

11

CONCLUDING COMMENTS

In spite of the difficulties inherent in obtaining reliable statistics about death by suicide in young people, and the likelihood that suicide is considerably underreported, sufficient evidence is available to suggest that among children suicide is very rare, whereas among adolescents the incidence of suicide is a significant problem, with rates increasing markedly throughout the teenage years. Although the numbers of suicides are relatively small, especially compared with adults, suicide is one of the major causes of death in this relatively healthy population. In recent years the rates of suicide among older adolescents have shown a disturbing increase in many countries, especially the United States. In all countries for which data are available, suicide rates among boys outnumber those among girls. The methods used for suicide appear, at least in part, to reflect availability; for example, firearms are often used in the United States while self-poisoning is more common elsewhere. In general, violent methods are used more by boys while self-poisoning is the predominant method among girls.

Unraveling the causes of suicide in young people is a difficult task, largely because of the necessarily retrospective nature of such inquiry. Family disruption and rejection by parents are common background features, with a break in an important relationship, disciplinary crises, isolation, lack of support, and depression and hopelessness being frequent precipitants.

Explanations for the recent increase in suicidal deaths among older teenagers can only be speculative. It has been postulated that the increase in broken homes with consequent loss of supports, changing attitudes to suicide, media reporting of suicidal deaths, and the increased use of psychotropic medication and of illicit drugs may all have played a part. The escalation in nonfatal self-poisoning may be another important contributory factor.

Child and adolescent suicide can have serious consequences for family members and friends, and these may lead to chronic problems including parental depression, marital disharmony, and difficulties in the management of other children. Counseling for the families of young suicides is extremely important and an approach to this has been suggested.

Attempted suicide is also relatively rare in children under the age of 12. Thereafter the rates increase steadily with age, especially among girls, who are far more at risk of making attempts than are boys. During the late 1960s and early 1970s, attempted suicide increased to almost epidemic proportions among adolescents, and the incidence continued to rise although less dramatically during the mid and later 1970s. A considerable amount is known about the characteristics of adolescent suicide attempters, especially the disturbed upbringing and family relations experienced by the majority. We know much about their problems and the factors that precipitate their suicide attempts. However, we are only just beginning to understand the complex motivational aspects of this behavior. Although the outcome in the majority of cases is good, a significant number make repeat attempts, and there is some evidence to suggest that the long-term risk of death by suicide is relatively high, especially among boys. If the morbidity and mortality in this minority of individuals is to be prevented, a better understanding of the motives that drive them seems essential.

Unfortunately, the management of young people who make attempts often appears to be inadequate. A very careful assessment is necessary in each case, preferably in the general hospital, and should include interviews with relatives and friends. Arrangements for aftercare need to be flexible, taking the adolescent's expressed needs firmly into account. A few cases will require inpatient psychiatric hospital treatment. Substantially more may benefit from outpatient or home-based counseling, in which other family members are involved where appropriate. Some young attempters can be returned to the care of their family doctor without further aftercare arrangements.

Prevention of child and adolescent suicidal behavior is an urgent task. Doctors, other health professionals and teachers play an important role in identifying those most at risk, but this is often difficult because their characteristics are shared by many more individuals who will not carry out suicidal acts. The task is probably better conceptualized in terms of helping young people develop their coping skills. Reduction in availability of dangerous methods that might be used for suicide should also be seriously considered. The media reporting of suicidal deaths by young people requires reappraisal. Suicide prevention agencies are of uncertain value, although an encouraging report has recently appeared in the United States suggesting that they have an important role in the prevention of suicides among young women. Common sense dictates that the development of well-organized and readily available helping agencies for young people must be encouraged.

There is obviously considerable room for further research into suicidal behavior among young people. First, more needs to be known about the motivational aspects; for example, it is unclear whether adolescent suicide attempters differ from other adolescents in their coping responses to stressful events. Second, there is a remarkable absence of research into the effectiveness of different forms of aftercare following suicide attempts by young people. Third, more information is required about both the short and long-term outcome of suicide attempts, especially the subsequent social adjustment and psychiatric morbidity, and the incidence of repeated attempts and eventual suicide. Finally, in terms of prevention of both attempted suicide and completed suicide by children and adolescents, we are only at the stage of conjecturing about possible strategies rather than being able to offer firm guidelines based on research findings.

FURTHER READING

The following books of relevance to suicidal behavior, especially among young people, may also be of interest to the reader.

Diekstra, R., & Hawton, K. (Eds.). (1986). *Suicide in adolescence.* The Hague: Martinus Nijhoff.

Hawton, K., & Catalan, J. (1982). *Attempted suicide: A practical guide to its nature and management.* Oxford: Oxford University Press.

Jacobs, G. (1971). *Adolescent suicide.* New York: Wiley-Interscience.

Kreitman, N. (Ed.). (1977). *Parasuicide.* London: Wiley.

Morgan, H. G. (1979). *Death wishes? The understanding and management of deliberate self-harm.* Chichester: Wiley.

REFERENCES

Adelstein, A., & Mardon, C. (1975). Suicides 1961-74. *Population Trends* (No. 2). London: Her Majesty's Stationery Office.

Anderson, L. S. (1981). Notes on the linkage between the sexually abused child and the suicidal adolescent. *Journal of Adolescence, 4,* 157-162.

Atkinson, M. W., Kessel, N., & Dalgaard, J. B. (1975). The comparability of suicide rates. *British Journal of Psychiatry, 127,* 247-256.

Bagley, C. R. (1968). The evaluation of a suicide prevention scheme by an ecological method. *Social Science and Medicine, 2,* 1-14.

Bagley, C. R. (1975). Suicidal behaviour and suicidal ideation in adolescents: A problem for counsellors in education. *British Journal of Guidance and Counselling, 3,* 190-208.

Bancroft, J., Hawton, K., Simkin, S., Kingston, B., Cumming, C., & Whitwell, D. (1979). The reasons people give for taking overdoses: A further enquiry. *British Journal of Medical Psychology, 52,* 353-365.

Bancroft, J., & Marsack, P. (1977). The repetitiveness of self-poisoning and self-injury. *British Journal of Psychiatry, 131,* 294-299.

Bancroft, J., Skrimshire, A., Casson, J., Harvard-Watts, O., & Reynolds, F. (1977). People who deliberately poison or injure themselves: Their problems and their contacts with helping agencies. *Psychological Medicine, 7,* 289-303.

Bancroft, J., Skrimshire, A., Reynolds, F., Simkin, S., & Smith, J. (1975). Self-poisoning and self-injury in the Oxford area: Epidemiological aspects 1969-73. *British Journal of Preventive and Social Medicine, 29,* 170-177.

Banks, M. H., & Jackson, P. R. (1982). Unemployment and risk of minor psychiatric disorder in young people: Cross-sectional and longitudinal evidence. *Psychological Medicine, 12,* 789-798.

Barraclough, B., Bunch, J., Nelson, B., & Sainsbury, P. (1974). A hundred cases of suicide: Clinical aspects. *British Journal of Psychiatry, 25,* 355-373.

Barraclough, B., Shepherd, D., & Jennings, C. (1977). Do newspaper reports of coroners' inquests incite people to commit suicide? *British Journal of Psychiatry, 131,* 528-532.

Barter, J. T., Swaback, D. O., & Todd, D. (1968). Adolescent suicide attempts: A follow-up study of hospitalized patients. *Archives of General Psychiatry, 19,* 523-527.

Bartolucci, G., & Drayer, C. S. (1973). An overview of crisis intervention in the emergency rooms of general hospitals. *American Journal of Psychiatry, 130,* 953-960.

Beck, A. T., Beck, R., & Kovacs, M. (1975). Classification of suicidal behavior: I. Quantifying intent and medical lethality. *American Journal of Psychiatry, 132,* 285-287.

Beck, A. T., Kovacs, M., & Weissman, A. (1975). Hopelessness and suicidal behavior. An overview. *Journal of the American Medical Association, 234,* 1146-1149.

Beck, A. T., Rush, A. J., Shaw, B. F., & Emery, G. (1979). *Cognitive therapy of depression.* New York: Guilford.

Beck, A. T., Schuyler, R. D., & Herman, J. (1974). Development of suicidal intent scales. In A. T. Beck, H.L.P. Resnick, & D. J. Lettieri (Eds.), *The prediction of suicide.* Illinois: Charles Press.

Beck, A. T., Ward, C. H., & Mendelson, M. (1961). An inventory for measuring depression. *Archives of General Psychiatry, 4,* 561-571.

Bergstrand, C. G., & Otto, U. (1962). Suicidal attempts in adolescence and childhood. *Acta Paediatrica, 51,* 17-26.

Bernstein, D. M. (1972). The distressed adolescent—pregnancy vs. suicide. In N. Morris (Ed.), *Psychosomatic medicine in obstetrics and gynaecology.* Basel: Karger.

Bollen, K. A., & Phillips, D. P. (1982). Imitative suicides: A national study of the effects of television news stories. *American Sociological Review, 47,* 802-809.

Breed, W. (1970). The Negro and fatalistic suicide. *Pacific Sociological Review, 13,* 156-162.

Brenner, M. H., & Mooney, A. (1983). Unemployment and health in the context of economic change. *Social Science and Medicine, 17,* 1125-1138.

Brooke, E. M. (1975). Suicide and the young. *World Health Organization Chronicle, 29,* 193-198.

Brown, G. W., & Harris, T. (1978). *Social origins of depression.* London: Tavistock.

Buglass, D., & Horton, J. (1974). A scale for predicting subsequent suicidal behaviour. *British Journal of Psychiatry, 124,* 573-578.

Buglass, D., & McCulloch, J. W. (1970). Further suicidal behaviour: The development and validation of predictive scales. *British Journal of Psychiatry, 116,* 483-491.

Calhoun, L. G., Selby, J. W., & Faulstich, M. E. (1980). Reactions of the parents of the child suicide: A study of social impressions. *Journal of Consulting and Clinical Psychology, 48,* 535-536.

Calhoun, L. G., Selby, J. W., & Faulstich, M. E. (1982). The aftermath of childhood suicide: Influences on the perception of the parents. *Journal of Community Psychology, 10,* 250-253.

Cantwell, D. P., & Carlson, G. (1979). Problems and prospects in the study of childhood depression. *Journal of Nervous and Mental Disease, 167,* 523-529.

Carlson, G. A., & Cantwell, D. P. (1982). Suicidal behavior and depression in children and adolescents. *Journal of the American Academy of Child Psychiatry, 21,* 361-368.

Carpenter, R. G. (1959). Statistical analysis of suicide and other mortality rates of students. *British Journal of Preventive and Social Medicine, 13,* 163-174.

Catalan, J., & Gath, D. H. (1985). Benzodiazepines in general practice: The time for a decision. *British Medical Journal.*

Catalan, J., Marsack, P., Hawton, K. E., Whitwell, D., Fagg, J., & Bancroft, J.H.J. (1980). Comparison of doctors and nurses in the assessment of deliberate self-poisoning patients. *Psychological Medicine, 10,* 483-491.

Chia, B. H. (1979). Suicide of the young in Singapore. *Annals of the Academy of Medicine, 8,* 262-268.

Children and parasuicide. (1981). *British Medical Journal, 283,* 337-338.

Chiles, J. A., Miller, M. L., & Cox, G. G. (1980). Depression in an adolescent delinquent population. *Archives of General Psychiatry, 37,* 1179-1186.

Choquet, M., Facy, F., & Davidson, F. (1980). Suicide and attempted suicide among adolescents in France. In R.D.T. Farmer & S. Hirsch (Eds.), *The suicide syndrome.* London: Cambridge University Press.

Chowdhury, N., Hicks, R. C., & Kreitman, N. (1973). Evaluation of an aftercare service for parasuicide (attempted suicide) patients. *Social Psychiatry, 8,* 67-81.

Clarkin, J. F., Friedman, R. C., Hurt, S. W., Corn, R., & Aronoff, M. (1984). Affective and character pathology of suicidal adolescents and young adult in-patients. *Journal of Clinical Psychiatry, 45,* 19-22.

Cluster phenomenon of young suicides raises "contagion theory." (1984, March 11). *Washington Post.*

Cohen-Sandler, R., Berman, A. L., & King, R. A. (1982). Life stress and symptomatology: Determinants of suicidal behavior in children. *Journal of the American Academy of Child Psychiatry, 21,* 178-186.

Connell, P. H. (1965). Suicidal attempts in childhood and adolescence. In J. G. Howell (Ed.), *Modern perspectives in child psychiatry.* Edinburgh: Oliver and Boyd.

Cosand, B. J., Bourque, L. B., & Kraus, J. F. (1982). Suicide among adolescents in Sacramento County, California 1950-1979. *Adolescence, 17,* 917-930.

Cresswell, P. A., & Smith, G. A. (1968). *Student suicide: A study in social integration.* Cambridge: Private publication.

Davidson, D.G.D., & Eastham, W. N. (1966). Acute liver necrosis following overdose of paracetamol. *British Medical Journal, 2,* 497-499.

Davidson, F., & Choquet, M. (1981). *Le suicide de l'adolescent: Etude epidemiologique et statistique.* Paris: Les Editions ESF.

Dorpat, T. L., Jackson, J. K., & Ripley, H. S. (1965). Broken homes and attempted suicide. *Archives of General Psychiatry, 12,* 213-216.

Douglas, J. D. (1967). *The social meanings of suicide.* Princeton: Princeton University Press.

Dublin, L. J. (1963). *Suicide: A sociological and statistical study.* New York: Ronald.

Durkheim, E. (1951). *Suicide.* New York: Free Press. (Original work published 1897).

Eisenberg, L. (1980). Adolescent suicide: On taking arms against a sea of troubles. *Pediatrics, 66,* 315-320.

Ewing, C. P. (1978). *Crisis intervention as psychotherapy.* New York: Oxford University Press.

Fogelman, K. (1976). *Britain's sixteen year olds.* London: National Children's Bureau.

Fox, K., & Weissman, M. (1975). Suicide attempts and drugs: Contradiction between method and intent. *Social Psychiatry, 10,* 31-38.

Fox, R. (1975). The suicide drop—why? *Royal Society of Health Journal, 1,* 9-20.

Francis, L. J. (1984). *Young and unemployed.* London: Costello.

Frederick, C. J. (1978). Current trends in suicidal behavior in the United States. *American Journal of Psychotherapy, 32,* 172-200.

Friedrich, W., Reams, R., & Jacobs, J. (1982). Depression and suicidal ideation in early adolescents. *Journal of Youth and Adolescence, 11,* 403-407.

Gardner, R., Hanka, R., O'Brien, V. C., Page, A.J.F., & Rees, R. (1977). Psychological and social evaluation in cases of deliberate self-poisoning admitted to a general hospital. *British Medical Journal, ii,* 1567-1570.

Garfinkel, B. D., Froese, A., & Golombek, H. (1979). Suicidal behaviour in a paediatric population. In *Proceedings of the 10th International Congress for Suicide Prevention and Crisis Intervention,* 305-312.

Garfinkel, B. D., & Golombek, H. (1983). Suicidal behavior in adolescence. In H. Golombek & B. D. Garfinkel (Eds.), *The adolescent & mood disturbance.* New York: International University Press.

Gazzard, B. G., Davis, M., Spooner, J., & Williams, R. (1976). Why do people use paracetamol for suicide? *British Medical Journal, i,* 212-213.

Gibbons, J. S., Butler, P., Urwin, P., & Gibbons, J. L. (1978). Evaluation of a social work service for self-poisoning patients. *British Journal of Psychiatry, 133,* 111-118.

Goldacre, M., & Hawton, K. (1985). Repetition of self-poisoning and subsequent death in adolescents who take overdoses. *British Journal of Psychiatry, 146,* 395-398.

Goldney, R. D., & Katsikitis, M. (1983). Cohort analysis of suicide rates in Australia. *Archives of General Psychiatry, 40,* 71-74.

Green, A. H. (1978). Self-destructive behavior in battered children. *American Journal of Psychiatry, 135,* 579-582.

Guze, S., & Robins, E. (1970). Suicide and primary affective disorders. *British Journal of Psychiatry, 117,* 437-438.

Haldane, J. D., & Haider, I. (1967). Attempted suicide in children and adolescents. *British Journal of Clinical Practice, 21,* 587-589.

Hassan, R. (1983). *A way of dying: Suicide in Singapore.* Kuala Lumpur: Oxford University Press.

Hatton, C. L., & Valente, S. M. (1981). Bereavement group for parents who suffered suicidal loss of a child. *Suicide and Life-Threatening Behavior, 11,* 141-150.

Hawton, K. (1978). Deliberate self-poisoning and self-injury in the psychiatric hospital. *British Journal of Medical Psychology, 51,* 253-259.

Hawton, K., Bancroft, J., Catalan, J., Kingston, B., Stedeford, A., & Welch, N. (1981). Domiciliary and out-patient treatment of self-poisoning patients by medical and non-medical staff. *Psychological Medicine, 11,* 169-177.

Hawton, K., & Blackstock, E. (1976). General practice aspects of self-poisoning and self-injury. *Psychological Medicine, 6,* 571-575.

Hawton, K., & Catalan, J. (1982). *Attempted suicide: A practical guide to its nature and management.* Oxford: Oxford University Press.

Hawton, K., Cole, D., O'Grady, J., & Osborn, M. (1982). Motivational aspects of deliberate self-poisoning in adolescents. *British Journal of Psychiatry, 141,* 286-291.

Hawton, K., Crowle, J., Simkin, S., & Bancroft, J. (1978). Attempted suicide and suicide among Oxford University students. *British Journal of Psychiatry, 132,* 506-509.

Hawton, K., Gath, D. H., & Smith, E.B.O. (1979). Management of attempted suicide in Oxford. *British Medical Journal, 2,* 1040-1042.

Hawton, K., & Goldacre, M. (1982). Hospital admissions for adverse effects of medicinal agents (mainly self-poisoning) among adolescents in the Oxford region. *British Journal of Psychiatry, 141,* 106-170.

Hawton, K., Marsack, P., & Fagg, J. (1981). The attitude of psychiatrists to deliberate self-poisoning: Comparison with physicians and nurses. *British Journal of Medical Psychology, 54,* 341-347.

Hawton, K., O'Grady, J., Osborn, M., & Cole, D. (1982). Adolescents who take overdoses: Their characteristics, problems and contacts with helping agencies. *British Journal of Psychiatry, 140,* 118-123.

Hawton, K., Osborn, M., O'Grady, J., & Cole, D. (1982). Classification of adolescents who take overdoses. *British Journal of Psychiatry, 140,* 124-131.

Hawton, K., Roberts, J., & Goodwin, G. (1985). The risk of child abuse among attempted suicide mothers with young children. *British Journal of Psychiatry, 146,* 486-489.

Headlam, H. K., Goldsmith, J., Hanenson, I. B., & Rauh, J. L. (1979). Demographic characteristics of adolescents with self-poisoning. A survey of 235 instances in Cincinnati, Ohio. *Clinical Pediatrics, 18,* 147-154.

Hellon, C. P., & Solomon, M. I. (1980). Suicide and age in Alberta, Canada, 1951 to 1977: The changing profile. *Archives of General Psychiatry, 37,* 505-510.

Herzog, A., & Resnik, H.L.P. (1967). A clinical study of parental response to adolescent death by suicide with recommendations for approaching the survivors. In *Proceedings of the 4th International Conference of Suicide Prevention.* Los Angeles: Delmar.

Holding, T. A., Buglass, D., Duffy, J. C., & Kreitman, N. (1977). Parasuicide in Edinburgh—a seven-year review 1968-74. *British Journal of Psychiatry, 130,* 534-543.

Holinger, P. C. (1978). Adolescent suicide: An epidemiological study of recent trends. *American Journal of Psychiatry, 135,* 754-756.

Igu, M. (1981). Suicide of Japanese youth.*Suicide and Life-threatening Behaviour, 11,* 17-30.

Innes, J. M. (1980). Suicide and the Samaritans. *Lancet, i,* 1138-1139.

Jacobs, G. (1971). *Adolescent suicide.* New York: Wiley-Interscience.

Jacobziner, H. (1965). Attempted suicide in adolescence. *Journal of the American Medical Association, 161,* 101-105.

James, D., & Hawton, K. (1985). Deliberate self-poisoning: Explanations and attitudes in patients and significant others. *British Journal of Psychiatry, 146,* 481-485.

Jennings, C., Barraclough, B. M., & Moss, J. R. (1978). Have the Samaritans lowered the suicide rate? A controlled study. *Psychological Medicine, 8,* 413-422.

Kashani, J. H., McGee, R. O, Clarkson, S. E., Anderson, J. C., Walton, L. A., Williams, S., Silva, P. A., Robins, A. J., Cytryn, L., & McKnew, D. H. (1983). Depression in a sample of 9-year old children. *Archives of General Psychiatry, 40,* 1217-1223.

Kass, D. J., Silvers, F. M., & Abroms, G. M. (1972). Behavioral group treatment of hysteria. *Archives of General Psychiatry, 26,* 42-50.

Kazdin, A. E., French, N. H., Unis, A. S., Esveldt-Dawson, K., & Sherick, R. B. (1983). Hopelessness, depression, and suicidal intent among psychiatrically disturbed in-patient children. *Journal of Consulting and Clinical Psychology, 51,* 504-510.

Koocher, P. G. (1974). Talking with children about death. *American Journal of Orthopsychiatry, 44,* 404-411.

Kosky, R. (1982). Suicide and attempted suicide among Australian children. *Medical Journal of Australia, 1,* 124-126.

Kosky, R. (1983). Childhood suicidal behaviour. *Journal of Child Psychology and Psychiatry, 24,* 457-468.

Kovacs, M., & Beck, A. T. (1977). An empirical clinical approach to a definition of childhood depression. In J. G. Schulterbrandt & A. Raskin (Eds.), *Depression in children: Diagnosis, treatment, and conceptual models.* New York: Raven Press.

Kreitman, N. (Ed.). (1977). *Parasuicide.* London: Wiley.

Kreitman, N. (1982). How useful is the prediction of suicide following parasuicide? In J. Wilmott & J. Mendelwicz (Eds.), *New trends in suicide prevention.* Basel: Karger.

Kreitman, N., & Schreiber, M. (1979). Parasuicide in young Edinburgh women, 1968-75. *Psychological Medicine, 9,* 469-479.

Kreitman, N., Smith, P., & Tan, E-S. (1970). Attempted suicide as language: An empirical study. *British Journal of Psychiatry, 116,* 465-473.

Leese, S. M. (1969). Suicide behavior in twenty adolescents. *British Journal of Psychiatry, 115*, 479-480.

Lester, D. (1974). Effect of suicide prevention centers on suicide rates in the United States. *Health Services Reports, 89*, 37-39.

Levenson, M., & Neuringer, C. (1971). Problem-solving behaviour in suicidal adolescents. *Journal of Consulting and Clinical Psychology, 37*, 433-436.

Liberman, R. P., & Eckman, T. (1981). Behavior therapy vs. insight-orientated therapy for repeated suicide attempters. *Archives of General Psychiatry, 38*, 1126-1130.

Litt, I. F., Cuskey, W. R., & Rudd, S. (1983). Emergency room evaluation of the adolescent who attempts suicide: Compliance with follow-up. *Journal of Adolescent Health Care, 4*, 106-108.

Lukianowicz, N. (1968). Attempted suicide in children. *Acta Psychiatrica Scandinavica, 44*, 415-435.

McAnarney, E. R. (1979). Adolescent and young adult suicide in the United States—a reflection of societal unrest? *Adolescence, 14*, 765-774.

McCarthy, P. D., & Walsh, D. (1975). Suicide in Dublin: I. The under-reporting of suicide and the consequences for national statistics. *British Journal of Psychiatry, 126*, 301-308.

McIntire, M. S., & Angle, C. R. (1973). Psychological "biopsy" in self-poisoning of children and adolescents. *American Journal of Diseases of Children, 126*, 42-46.

McClure, G.M.G. (1984). Trends in suicide rate for England and Wales, 1975-80. *British Journal of Psychiatry, 144*, 119-126.

McClure, G.M.G. (1984). Recent trends in suicide amongst the young. *British Journal of Psychiatry, 144*, 134-138.

Margolin, N. L., & Teicher, J. D. (1968). Thirteen adolescent male suicide attempts. *Journal of the American Academy of Child Psychiatry, 7*, 296-315.

Mattsson, A., Seese, L. R., & Hawkins, J. W. (1969). Suicidal behavior as a child psychiatric emergency. *Archives of General Psychiatry, 20*, 100-109.

Meares, R., Mendelsohn, F.A.O., & Milgrom-Friedman, J. (1981). A sex difference in the seasonal variation of suicide rate: A single cycle for men, two cycles for women. *British Journal of Psychiatry, 138*, 321-325.

Mehr, M., Zeltzer, L. K., & Robinson, R. (1981). Continued self-destructive behaviors in adolescent suicide attempters: Part 1. *Journal of Adolescent Health Care, 1*, 269-274.

Mehr, M., Zeltzer, L, K., & Robinson, R. (1982). Continued self-destructive behaviors in adolescent suicide attemptors: Part II, a pilot study. *Journal of Adolescent Health Care, 2*, 183-187.

Miller, H. L., Coombs, D. W., Leeper, J. D., & Barton, S. N. (1984). An analysis of the effects of suicide prevention facilities on suicide rates in the United States. *American Journal of Public Health, 74*, 340-343.

Miller, J., Sakinofsky, I., & Streiner, D. L. (1979). The family and social dynamics of adolescent parasuicide. In *Proceedings of the 10th International Conference for Suicide Prevention and Crisis Intervention*, Ottawa.

Mills, J., Williams, C., Sale, I., Perkin, G., & Henderson, S. (1974). The epidemiology of self-poisoning in Hobart, 1968-1972. *Australian and New Zealand Journal of Psychiatry, 8*, 167-172.

Minuchin, S. (1974). *Families and family therapy*. London: Tavistock.

Minuchin, S., & Fishman, H. C. (1981). *Family therapy techniques*. Boston: Harvard University Press.

Morgan, H. G. (1979). *Death wishes? The understanding and management of deliberate self-harm.* Chichester: Wiley.

Mulcock, D. (1955). Juvenile suicide: a study of suicide and attempted suicide over a 16 year period. *Medical Officer,* 155-160.

Murphy, G. E., & Wetzel, R. D. (1980). Suicide risk by birth cohort in the United States, 1949 to 1974. *Archives of General Psychiatry, 37,* 519-523.

Nardini-Maillard, D., & Ladame, F. G. (1980). The results of a follow-up study of suicidal adolescents. *Journal of Adolescence, 3,* 253-260.

National Center for Health Statistics (1984). *Monthly Vital Statistics Report, 1981* (33, No. 3, June 22). (includes personal communication concerning earlier reports)

Newson-Smith, J.G.B., & Hirsch, S. R. (1979). A comparison of social workers and psychiatrists in evaluating parasuicide. *British Journal of Psychiatry, 134,* 335-342.

O'Brien, J. P. (1977). Increase in suicide attempts by drug ingestion: The Boston experience, 1964-1974. *Archives of General Psychiatry, 34,* 1165-1169.

Offer, D., & Barglow, P. (1960). Adolescent and young adult self-mutilation incidents in a general psychiatric hospital. *Archives of General Psychiatry, 3,* 102-112.

Office of Population Censuses and Surveys. (1974-1982). *Mortality Statistics:* Cause. London: Her Majesty's Stationery Office. (includes personal communication)

Ogden, M., Specter, M. I., & Hill, C. A. (1970). Suicides and homicides among Indians. *Public Health Reports, 85,* 75-80.

Oliver, R. G., & Hetzel, B. S. (1973). An analysis of recent trends in suicide rates in Australia. *International Journal of Epidemiology, 2,* 91-101.

Oliver, R. G., Kaminski, Z., Tudor, K., & Hetzel, B. S. (1971). The epidemiology of attempted suicide as seen in the casualty department, Alfred Hospital, Melbourne. *Medical Journal of Australia, 1,* 833-839.

Orbach, I., Carlson, G., Feshbach, S., Glaubman, M., & Gross, Y. (1983). Attraction and repulsion by life and death in suicidal and in normal children. *Journal of Consulting and Clinical Psychology, 51,* 661-670.

Otto, U. (1972). Suicidal acts by children and adolescents. *Acta Psychiatrica Scandinavica, Supplement 233.*

Ovenstone, I.M.K. (1973). A psychiatric approach to the diagnosis of suicide and its effect upon the Edinburgh statistics. *British Journal of Psychiatry, 12,* 315-321.

Parker, A. (1981). The meaning of attempted suicide to young parasuicides: A repertory grid study. *British Journal of Psychiatry, 139,* 306-312.

Parrish, H. M. (1957). Epidemiology of suicide among college students. *Yale Journal of Biology and Medicine, 29,* 585-595.

Paykel, E. S., Prusoff, B. A., & Myers, J. K. (1975). Suicide attempts and recent life events: A controlled comparison. *Archives of General Psychiatry, 32,* 327-333.

Piaget, J. (1960). *The child's concept of the world.* Patterson, NJ: Littlefield Adams.

Pierce, D. W. (1981). Predictive validation of a suicide intent scale. *British Journal of Psychiatry, 139,* 391-396.

Petzel, S. V., & Cline, D. W. (1978). Adolescent suicide: Epidemiological and biological aspects. *Adolescent Psychiatry, 6,* 239-266.

Pfeffer, C. R., Conte, H. R., Plutchik, R., & Jerrett, I. (1979). Suicidal behavior in latency-age children. *Journal of the American Academy of Child Psychiatry, 18,* 679-692.

Pfeffer, C. R., Conte, H. R., Plutchik, R., & Jerrett, I. (1980) Suicidal behavior in latency-age children: An out-patient population. *Journal of the American Academy of Child Psychiatry, 19,* 703-710.

Phillips, D. P. (1974). The influence of suggestion on suicide: Substantive and theoretical implications of the Werther effect. *American Sociological Review, 39,* 340-354.

Ramon, S., Bancroft, J.H.J., & Skrimshire, A. M. (1975). Attitudes towards self-poisoning among physicians and nurses in a general hospital. *British Journal of Psychiatry, 127,* 257-264.

Registrar General (1960-1973). *Statistical Review for England and Wales. Part I.* London: Her Majesty's Stationery Office.

Richman, J. (1979). The family therapy of attempted suicide. *Family Process, 18,* 131-142.

Roberts, J., & Hawton, K. (1980). Child abuse and attempted suicide. *British Journal of Psychiatry, 137,* 319-323.

Robins, E. (1981). *The final months: A study of the lives of 134 persons who committed suicide.* New York: Oxford University Press.

Rohn, R. D., Sarles, R. M., Kenny, T. J., Reynolds, B. J., & Head, F. P. (1977). Adolescents who attempt suicide. *Journal of Pediatrics, 90,* 636-638.

Rosen, L. W., & Thomas, M. A. (1984). Treatment techniques for chronic wrist cutters. *Journal of Behavior Therapy and Experimental Psychiatry, 15,* 33-36.

Rosenthal, P. A., & Rosenthal, S. (1984). Suicidal behaviour by pre-school children. *American Journal of Psychiatry, 141,* 520-525.

Rosenthal, R. J., Rinzler, C., & Klausner, E. (1972). Wrist-cutting syndrome: The meaning of a gesture. *American Journal of Psychiatry, 128,* 1363-1368.

Rudestam, K. E. (1977). The impact of suicide among the young. *Essence, 1,* 221-224.

Rudestam, K. E., & Imbroll, D. (1983). Societal reactions to a child's death by suicide. *Journal of Consulting and Clinical Psychology, 51,* 461-462.

Rumack, B. H. (1983). Acetaminophen overdose. *American Journal of Medicine, 75,* 104-112.

Sainsbury, P., & Barraclough, B. (1968). Differences between suicide rates. *Nature, 220,* 1252.

Sanborn, D. E., Sanborn, C. J., & Cimbolic, P. (1973). Two years of suicide: A study of adolescent suicide in New Hampshire. *Child Psychiatry and Human Development, 3,* 234-237.

Sathyavathi, K. (1975). Suicide among children in Bangalore. *Indian Journal of Paediatrics, 42,* 149-157.

Seiden, R. H. (1969). Suicide among youth. *Supplement to the Bulletin of Suicidology.*

Seiden, R. H. (1972). Why are suicides of young Blacks increasing? *H.S.M.H.A., Health Report, 87,* 3-8.

Shaffer, D. (1974). Suicide in childhood and early adolescence. *Journal of Child Psychology and Psychiatry, 15,* 275-291.

Shaffer, D., & Fisher, P. (1981). The epidemiology of suicide in children and young adolescents. *Journal of the American Academy of Child Psychiatry, 20,* 545-565.

Simpson, M. A. (1975). Self-mutilation in a general hospital setting. *Canadian Psychiatric Association Journal, 20,* 429-433.

Simpson, M. A. (1976). Self-mutilation. *British Journal of Hospital Medicine, 16,* 430-438.

Sims, L., & Ball, M. J. (1973). Suicide among university students. *Journal of the American College Health Association, 21,* 336-338.

Solomon, M. I., & Hellon, C. P. (1980). Suicide and age in Alberta, Canada, 1951-1977: A cohort analysis. *Archives of General Psychiatry, 37,* 511-513.

Stanley, E. J., & Barter, J. T., (1970). Adolescent suicidal behavior. *American Journal of Orthopsychiatry, 40,* 87-96.

Steinberg, D. (1983). *The clinical psychiatry of adolescence.* Chichester: Wiley.

Stengel, C., & Cook, N. G. (1958). *Attempted suicide: Its social significance and effects* (Maudsley Monograph No. Four). London: Oxford University Press.

Struve, F. A., Klein, D. F., & Saraf, K. R. (1972). Electroencephalographic correlates of suicide. *Archives of General Psychiatry, 27,* 363-365.

Taylor, E. A., Stansfield, S. A. (1984). Children who poison themselves: I. Clinical comparison with psychiatric controls, & II. Prediction of attendance for treatment. *British Journal of Psychiatry, 145,* 127-135.

Teicher, J. D., & Jacobs, J. (1966). Adolescents who attempt suicide: Preliminary findings. *American Journal of Psychiatry, 122,* 1248-1257.

Toolan, J. M. (1962). Depression in children and adolescents. *American Journal of Orthopsychiatry, 32,* 404-415.

Topol, P., & Reznikoff, N. (1982). Perceived peer and family relationships, hopelessness and locus of control as factors in adolescent suicide attempts. *Suicide and Life-Threatening Behavior, 12,* 141-150.

Trethowan, W. H. (1975). Pills for personal problems. *British Medical Journal, 3,* 749-751.

Tuckman, J., & Connon, H. E. (1962). Attempted suicide in adolescents. *American Journal of Psychiatry, 119,* 228-232.

U.S. Department of Health, Education and Welfare (1973). *Suicide, homicide, and alcoholism among American Indians: Guidelines for help* (Publication No (ADM) 74-42). Rockville, MD: Department of Health, Education and Welfare.

Walker, W. L. (1980). Intentional self-injury in school age children. *Journal of Adolescence, 3,* 217-228.

Weiner, I. W. (1969). The effectiveness of a suicide prevention program. *Mental Hygiene, 53,* 357-363.

Weissman, M. M. (1974). The epidemiology of suicide attempts, 1960 to 1971. *Archives of General Psychiatry, 30,* 737-746.

Wetzel, R. D. (1976). Hopelessness, depression, and suicidal intent. *Archives of General Psychiatry, 33,* 1069-1073.

Wexler, L., Weissman, M. M., & Kasl, S. V. (1978). Suicide attempts 1970-75: Updating a United States study and comparisons with international trends. *British Journal of Psychiatry, 132,* 180-185.

White, E., Elsom, B., & Prawat, R. (1978). Children's conceptions of death. *Child Development, 49,* 307-310.

White, H. C. (1974). Self-poisoning in adolescents. *British Journal of Psychiatry, 124,* 24-35.

Whitehead, P. C., Johnson, F. G., & Ferrence, R. (1973). Measuring the incidence of self-injury: Some methodological and design considerations. *American Journal of Orthopsychiatry, 43,* 142-148.

Worden, W. (1983). *Grief counselling and grief therapy.* London: Tavistock.

Zilboorg, G. (1936). Consideration on suicide with particular reference to that of the young. *American Journal of Orthopsychiatry, 7,* 15-35.

INDEX

ABOUT THE AUTHOR

Keith Hawton is a consultant psychiatrist in Oxford. During the past 12 years he has worked in the University Department of Psychiatry where he has gained extensive research and clinical experience in the field of suicidal behavior. He is also an authority on sexual disorders. In 1980 he received his D.M. from Oxford University for research concerning the treatment of people following suicide attempts. Previous books by him include *Attempted Suicide: A Practical Guide to its Nature and Management* with Dr. José Catalan, and *Sex Therapy: A Practical Guide.* He is a Fellow of Green College, Oxford.